MW01094765

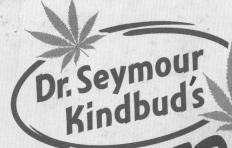

Dr. Seymour Kindbud's

STONER SNACKS

MORE THAN 100 RECIPES FOR SAVORY AND SWEET MEALS & MUNCHIES

13-Digit ISBN: 978-1604332148
10-Digit ISBN: 160433214X

This book may be ordered by mail from the publisher. Please include $2.99 for postage and handling.
Please support your local bookseller first!

Books published by Cider Mill Press Book Publishers are available at special discounts for bulk purchases in the United States by corporations, institutions, and other organizations. For more information, please contact the publisher.

Cider Mill Press Book Publishers
"Where good books are ready for press"
12 Port Farm Road
Kennebunkport, Maine 04046

Visit us on the Web!
www.cidermillpress.com

Cover Design by Bashan Aquart
Interior Design and Illustration: Doublemranch.com
All photographs courtesy of Shutterstock
Printed in China

1 2 3 4 5 6 7 8 9 0
First Edition

contents

INTRODUCTION

Cooking with cannabis is a whole new world. And now that you're holding **Stoner Snacks** in your hands you're about to enter it. When making the easy recipes in this book you'll find that within minutes you can be nibbling and noshing your way to a great high—deliciously too.

The sneaky part about cooking with weed is that you can get stoned anywhere at any time. At the movies? On a plane? While working? Sure. Your little home-baked hooch treats are your new BFF.

Indeed you can get a good buzz on from ingesting weed. It's a longer lasting high than you get from smoking it, but it takes longer to kick in than taking that first deep toke. So starting a little stoned makes the whole cooking process ever more enjoyable, too.

While you can pick off fresh leaves from your plants and add them to a vegetable stir-fry, I discovered the best way to wow with weed was to use it as an ingredient that gets distributed evenly through the whole dish. If your portion of the stir-fry didn't get any "special greens" you'd be out of luck, while the person next to you was high within minutes. But if you make Hooched Herb and Garlic Bread (page 37) with Bong Butter it's in each and every aromatic and ganga-filled morsel.

What carries the flavors in food is the fat, and when that fat has been infused with THC, the magical chemical that gives you the buzz from boom, Nirvana has been reached. Why roll a joint when you can get just as high from Cheeba Chocolate Coconut Bars (page 92) or Cheesy Cannabis Puffs (page 34)?

There are recipes for both sweet treats and savory snacks in this book. They're all fast to make and use mainly stuff you've got around, assuming your idea of a pantry is more than a receptacle for take-out menus, and you use your refrigerator to keep stuff cold instead of as a bookshelf or hamper.

It was way back in 1963—when I was still so young that pot to me was used most often in tandem with the word flower—when Bob Dylan wrote the immortal lyrics to "The Times They Are a-Changin." From the '60s to the end of the twentieth century, the highway to a high was smoking your dope. Rolling joysticks was a way of life, as it had been for centuries.

But not today. Dylan was right.

A big reason for "chewing your cheeba" and cooking with cannabis is that there are fewer and fewer places you can light up anything these days! It's time to face facts; the Health Nazis now rule the world. Who would have thought a few years ago that on a trip to Paris I couldn't have even a Gauloises hanging from my lower lip in a café?

Even when (note, I didn't write if) pot is legalized, you still won't be able to smoke it inside restaurants, libraries, or just about anywhere else. Getting "Eight Miles High" with "Puff the Magic Dragon" is going to become a thing of the past. And in all fairness, a joint has three times the amount of tar as a tobacco cigarette and produces more carbon monoxide. But, hey, there's none of that bad nicotine stuff in it.

You may think that cooking is hard, or that you'll wait for the panoply of pot snacks to appear on the market once it's legalized. But you're wrong. I was new to the world of cooking—cannabis and otherwise. And now I'm a kitchen geek.

Back in 2010 when I was researching **Green Weed**, my landmark book on organic methods of growing grass, I had both pet fish and pet rabbits for a few months because their poop contained so many great nutrients that I used it as a natural fertilizer. But then the fish became "floaters" and the bunnies ran away to do whatever bunnies do when they run away. They probably ran away to some cheap motel to make more bunnies.

So I needed to replace their "after-products" in my organic arsenal. I discovered that food waste—like eggshells dried in the oven and then ground up in the food processor—were even better than bunny poop for my plants! Ditto for onion peels and carrot trimmings, as well as the leftover grounds from the pot of coffee I needed to write intensely about growing pot.

But using these fertilizers was a bit complicated. With the fish and bunnies it was easy; I'd feed them through one end and use what they then put out the other end. But in order to have eggshells to grind, I first needed to do something with the eggs.

Not being wasteful is hot-wired into my DNA. Back in the sixteenth century kids learned that "willful waste makes woeful want," which then got abbreviated by whatever the eighteenth century version was of Twitter to "waste not, want not."

I couldn't eat breakfast more than three times a day, and if I put onions and carrots in my omelets they took too long to cook. And was there something I could do with a food processor other than grind eggshells?

Then I met this amazing woman, and she introduced me to something equally amazing—the World of Cooking! The inner chef in me was awakened, and this is one genie that will never go back into either the bottle or the bong. W.C. Fields once quipped that "a woman drove me to drink and I didn't even have the decency to thank her." Well, I thanked this woman, and I thank her again here. You know who you are, you vixen you!

I discovered cooking was fun! I really enjoyed it! And there were all sorts of innovative ways to meet the munchies when I was stoned. Instead of a bag of corn chips, I could make my own nachos. Instead of downing a pair of Hostess Twinkies I could whip up a chocolate cake. Cooking is part art and part science, and we all know how when you're high the artist in you dominates your personality.

For the year I was finishing **Green Weed** I was cooking when I was stoned, but not as a way to get stoned! That was the second Rubicon to cross in this quest. Thus, the seeds for this book on "gastronomic ganga" were planted as carefully as those for a tray of Sour Diesel.

All the dishes in this book have intense flavor. I'm not a namby-pamby kind of guy, and no one wants to eat something boring, even if the result will get you stoned. So these recipes have all been developed to deliver dynamite flavor but with short cooking times. After all, if you're not stoned when you cook them you will be soon after, and we know that flavor is what it's about.

Happy cooking!

Dr. Seymour Kindbud

chapter 1

BASICS OF THE POT PANTRY

This chapter is where all the fun begins. Once you've mastered how to make these foundation ingredients, all of which contain your cannabis, then your world of feeding your psyche while you're feeding your face begins.

While all the dishes in Stoner Snacks refer to these basic recipes, you can then transfer the knowledge learned here to any and all of your favorite recipes. Cooking with cannabis is where we're going in the future to reach our euphoric states, and it all begins here.

Also included in this chapter is a pithy historic discussion of cannabis so you can sound as phony as wine aficionados discussing it, plus a section on how ingesting it differs from the high you get when puffing it.

Like Alice through the looking glass, your world of ganga greatness starts here.

A Cavalcade of Cannabis Around the World

It's hard to believe when you're looking at a piece of rope made from hemp that the same vegetal material is what you smoke! In fact ganja is the Sanskrit word for hemp.

Hardy and versatile, all three species of cannabis plants (given fancy Latin names like cannabis sativa, cannabis indica, and cannabis ruderalis) grow in temperate zones all over the world. It has been a source of food, fiber, and medicine since ancient times, or at least for the 8,000 years we've been able to track it. And what an efficient plant it is! All parts of the plant—the leaves, buds, seeds, and even the stalks—are edible. To use the language of today, cannabis is a Wonder Food.

Those tricky devils in China were the first to recognize the medicinal virtues of weed and listed it as an analgesic more than 4,000 years ago, while the seeds from it are listed amongst boring crops like soybeans as an ancient grain. The old Chinese were really into their weed; in fact, a bag of it was found in a tomb that dates back about 3,000 years.

In the second century BCE a surgeon named Hua T'o created an anesthetic using a mixture of weed and wine. So we didn't invent that combo any more than we did most other things. And we know about this great discovery because by that time the Chinese also had paper made from hemp on which to write stuff. What a waste of weed!

Other old-timers in the cultivation of cannabis are natives of the Indian subcontinent and people in the Middle East. By about 1000 BCE these cultures were into recreational weed. The Vedic texts of Hinduism written between 2000 and 1500 BCE record that the god Shiva lived within a cannabis plant so it was a "sacred grass" to them.

Indians also turned it into a beverage, called bhang. It's a combination of milk or yogurt, pot, and ground almonds all mixed with spices. A glass was the equivalent of their "martini straight up shaken, not stirred" at the end of a day. "The mere sight of bhang cleanses as much sin as a thousand pilgrimages" is a passage included in one Hindu text. You'll find a simplified recipe for it on page 17, because it's also a great ingredient in cooking.

Indian spiritual leaders, called Saduha, use chewing the leaves to honor their pantheon of gods in the same way that coca leaves are used in South America. And on Buddha's path to enlightenment, all he ate was the cannabis plant, including its seeds. No wonder he was so enlightened, without even lighting up!

The great milestone credited to cannabis cooks in the Middle East is the invention of hash. For those of you new to "Cult of Cannabis," hashish is a resin made from the flowering tops of the female plant that is eventually pressed into small cakes.

While Arabic societies may not approve of drinking alcohol, they had no such prohibition on pot. Mahjoun, sweets made with honey laced with hash into which nuts and dried fruits are folded, date from the eleventh century, and 200 years later the Sufi sect had turned hash into a form of chewing gum and considered hashish to be a vital part of its mysticism. That explains why those dervish guys are so happy to spin in circles.

While kif, as it's called there, is a big recreational drug in Morocco, use of cannabis is not found that much in Africa. One exception is in what we now call the Congo, where warriors used it as a pep pill before battle.

In Western culture, both in Europe and in the New World, cannabis was a footnote rather than a main topic. The Greek historian Herodotus writes of how the nomadic Scythian tribe, who lived in what we now call parts of Iran and to the Russian steppes as well as along the north side of the Black Sea, would burn the seeds as part of funeral rite. "The smell of it made them drunk, just as wine does us," was his commentary. It appears that no one was bitching at those Scythians' funerals about the evils of second-hand smoke.

The Scythians also introduced cannabis to Northern Europe during their migratory travels; an urn was unearthed near Berlin that contains seeds and leaves dating from 500 BCE. Other tribes were also devotees of dope. There are pipes in the shapes of cups found within what is today Romania with residues of smoked seeds that date back to the Bronze Age.

Because cannabis didn't play a big role in Judeo-Christian religion or the cultures that spawned it, it wasn't appreciated much in the New World. It was likely brought to South America by the Spanish conquistadors, and in colonial America hemp was second only to cotton in importance as a crop. It was introduced to Jamestown, Virginia, in 1611 and Plymouth, Massachusetts, in 1632. But it was totally wasted by those uptight Puritans, who used it just to make cloth and rope from it. George Washington grew it at Mount Vernon, and Thomas Jefferson planted it at Monticello.

Finally, we find American pharmaceutical uses for cannabis reported when state-by-state bans began in the early twentieth century. But now we anticipate that everything old is going to be new again—including the legalization of cannabis.

We all know how creative we feel when we're stoned, and a bunch of creative Bohemian types in Paris celebrated weed. Called the Club de Hashischins, it was active from 1844 to 1849 in Paris, with a hangout in the Hotel de Lauzun on the Ile St. Louis. The members of the Club were the intellectual elite of the day including painter Eugene Delacroix and writers Alexandre Dumas, Theophile Gautier, and Charles Baudelaire. One member of the group was a noted psychiatrist of the day, Dr. Jacques-Joseph Moreau. He was the first to publish work on the effect of drugs on the central nervous system.

Different Strokes for Different Folks

What everyone finds during first forays of cooking with cannabis is that the high is definitely there, but it's different from the high you get when you're puffing. This section explains why.

The ingredient that gets you high on pot is Tetrahydrocannabinol, or delta 9 THC for short. While all parts of the plant contain this wonder substance, the buds have the highest level. The forms in which delta 9 THC are found in cannabis are many; they're called isomers, and at least fifty have been isolated of which only six are psychoactive. Some lead to euphoria, while others lead to relaxation, and some lead to drowsiness.

When you smoke weed and inhale deeply, the THC transfuses into your blood almost instantly thorough the thousands of capillaries located on the surface of the lungs. This reaction increases with how much time the smoke is in contact with the capillaries, which is why inhaled smoke should be held in for as long as possible without turning blue.

From these capillaries, the THC enters the bloodstream. It then makes a beeline right to the brain and links up with receptors waiting for it like horny sailors hitting port. This transmission from the lungs to the brain is almost instantaneous, which is why you get high so quickly. But it wears off once the THC molecules no longer bind to the receptors.

Eating weed is a more complex physiological trip. When eaten, the THC is turned into a THC metabolite in the liver and becomes a compound called 11-hydroxy-THC. The high from this THC derivative is actually more powerful than the lungs-to-brain high. But it starts slower. That's the bummer. But it also can last for up to five hours. That's the plus, and which is why cooking with cannabis brings a sense of gourmet enjoyment, both through the food in which its cooked and the total experience of savoring.

Elements of Cannabis Cookery

You know how oil and water don't mix? Well, neither does THC and water. The only way to get the chemical into your food is via fat. That's why you have to infuse either butter or oil with weed to get the effects.

Another fact of cooking fu is that you get the best results once the weed is heated. While you can add leaves from your pet plants to a salad, you'll get a much better buzz if you add them to a stir-fry instead.

Bong Butter

Bong Butter is the Mother's Milk of cannabis cookery. You can use it slathered on your toast at breakfast. You can sauté savory foods in it, and you can bake with it for sweet treats. The THC in the weed is transferred to the fat in the butter, and the water in which it's all boiling together keeps it from scorching.

I'm assuming that the usual amount per recipe is 2 tablespoons per person, and that translates into about 2 grams of weed per serving. Making Bong Butter is more a method and formula than a recipe, and you can do a few pounds of butter at a time; it keeps for a few weeks refrigerated or frozen for up to six months. But it never lasts that long in my house!

The formulation is 1 stick of unsalted butter (¼ pound) per ¼ to ½ ounce of weed. This recipe is for up to 1 pound of Bong Butter. Adding more water to the pan can scale it up.

Bring a few cups of water to a boil in a saucepan, and while the water is heating, grind up your weed in a special grinder reserved for this purpose, or in a mortar and pestle. Melt your butter in the boiling water, and stir in the ground weed. Reduce the heat to low, and cover the pan. Simmer for 2 hours, stirring it occasionally.

Strain the liquid into a bowl through a fine-mesh sieve lined with a few layers of cheesecloth or a few paper coffee filters. Let the liquid sit at room temperature until cool, and then cover it with plastic wrap and refrigerate it overnight, or until the butter on top of the liquid has formed a solid layer. There's no magic about overnight; but it does take up to eight hours, depending on how much you made.

Just pull off the solid stuff and throw out the liquid stuff. Voilà! You've got a stash of Bong Butter.

You can also cook the Bong Butter in a slow cooker set on Low. It takes forever for water and butter to come to a boil in the slow cooker, so I advocate doing that on top of the stove and transferring it. The advantage of a slow cooker is that you never have to worry that the water will boil away because it cooks at such a low temperature, so you can leave the house. But never lift the lid of a slow cooker while it's working. Look inside by jiggling the lid to clear the condensation.

Augmented Oil

You'll really get off on the aromatics from cooking this oil. It needs many hours of low heat, so it fills the kitchen with a really mellow "grassy" smell as it finishes cooking. I usually make two versions, one with olive oil for savory cooking and salad dressings and the other made with a flavorless oil like peanut oil or canola oil; use that version if you don't want the olive oil flavor.

The best way to make the oil is in a slow cooker. You can use weed trimmings as well as buds, and you need ³/₄ ounce to 1 ounce per 1 cup of oil. Combine the oil and pot in the slow cooker, and set it on low. Cook it for 10 to 12 hours, stirring after about 6 hours.

If you don't have a slow cooker, you can make it in a saucepan on top of the stove. Heat the oil to a temperature of 200ºF, and then stir in the weed. Keep it at that temperature for 6 to 8 hours.

Strain the oil through a fine mesh sieve; don't worry if a little of the solids get through. Then store it either in a cool and dark place or—even better—in the refrigerator. The colder the temperature the better for the oil, although you might have to let it sit out if it hardens.

Amazing Mayo

This high-test mayo can make that bowl of tuna salad you're bringing to the office for lunch a lot more interesting, and you can also use it in salad dressings or smeared on bread for a sandwich. The basis of it is Augmented Oil, and making it in a blender is incredibly easy. This recipe makes two cups of mayo, which is a good supply to keep on hand.

1 large egg, at room temperature
2 large egg yolks, at room temperature
½ teaspoon mustard powder
2 tablespoons lemon juice or more to taste
2 cups Augmented Oil (page 15)
Salt and freshly ground black pepper to taste

YIELD: 2¼ cups
ACTIVE TIME: 10 minutes
START TO FINISH: 10 minutes

1. Combine egg, egg yolks, mustard powder, and lemon juice in a blender. Blend at high speed for 45 seconds.

2. With the motor running, remove the stopper from the top of the blender, and begin to add oil 1 teaspoon at a time until half of the oil is added and the sauce is very thick. Scrape down the sides of the blender beaker.

3. Add remaining oil in 1 tablespoon portions, beating well between each addition. Season to taste with salt and pepper, and add more lemon juice, if desired.

NOTE: The mayonnaise can be made up to 5 days in advance and refrigerated, tightly covered.

Bhang Booster

In India bhang is a drink unto itself. This variation made with evaporated milk so that it has a long life refrigerated is used as an ingredient in many recipes. Because it's heated during the infusing cycle, it can be used cold in dishes and deliver its desired buzz. There's enough fat in regular evaporated milk for all the THC goodies to find a good home, so don't buy any low-fat versions.

Combine 1 (12-ounce) can of evaporated milk with 1/2 ounce of pulverized weed in a small saucepan. Bring it to a simmer over medium heat, stirring it occasionally. Reduce the heat to low, and simmer for 10 minutes. Strain it through a paper coffee filter. Press hard to get as much liquid out of the weed as possible. Then refrigerate the bhang.

In addition to being soluble in oil, THC also does well in booze, which can be used in cooking too, or just poured over some ice cubes. The formulation for Booze with Buzz is 1/4 ounce of weed per 3 ounces of liquor.

Pound the weed into a powder with a mortar and pestle, and soak it overnight in water. This gets rid of any dirt on the weed, but doesn't take away from the THC. Then drain it off and pour booze over it in a little jar. Hide the jar in a cool dark place (like alongside your vanilla extract), and let it mellow for 2 weeks, shaking it every day.

Strain it through a paper coffee filter. Press hard to get as much liquid out of the weed as possible. Then store it refrigerated. Like all pot-potent foods, this has to be heated to activate its goodies, but you'll find lots of ways to do that later in this book.

Keeping Track of Your Treats

As already mentioned, you don't get an instant buzz with cannabis cookery. That's why I suggest smoking a bit as you're cooking, if you're in an environment where that's possible.

If not, don't keep eating more than a portion of any of these recipes thinking it will bring the high on faster. It won't. But you may not remember much once the souped-up THC kicks in. Also, the cannabis creations should be limited to one or two dishes in the course of a meal. Not every food should contain Bong Butter or Augmented Oil any more than you should make a joint that's two feet long and smoke it to the nub in one sitting.

Easy does it!

chapter 2

DIPPITY DO AND SIMPLE SAVORIES

I know there are times that all you want is something sweet, and in this case the sweets in chapters 4 and 5 get you into a euphoric state as well as meeting your needs for munchies. But then there are times you're craving garlic instead of gingerbread, or chiles instead of chocolate.

Savory snacks are the recipes you'll find in this chapter. There are dips to spread on crackers or dip with veggies (it's amazing how much more noise it creates to chew a carrot when you're stoned!). Then there are hot and cold snacks, many of them made with some sort of gooey and yummy cheese, and then breads that can be a treat all their own.

The Crudité Collection

What differentiates a dip from a bruschetta topping is the consistency. Dips are smooth, and bruschetta toppings are chunky. But many of the recipes in this chapter can be used interchangeably with vegetables or bread. Slices of cucumber or small cups made from leaves of iceberg or leaf lettuce are great additions to a mix if people are on low-calorie or gluten-free diets.

The basket of vegetables served with dips—now called crudités—can be as simple as carrots and celery, but whatever the contents, the key is to arrange it artistically. I line a low basket with plastic wrap, and then cover the plastic with lettuce leaves; an alternative is to use an Asian vegetable steamer.

Vegetables such as cauliflower, string beans, and broccoli should be blanched before serving. But rather than dirty a pot, it's more efficient to accomplish this in a microwave. Steam the vegetables for 1 to 2 minutes, then plunge them into ice water to stop the cooking action. Drain, and you're ready to arrange.

If you're serving crudités at a large party, you can prepare them in advance using this trick: Cut up and/or steam your vegetables and wrap them in damp paper towels. Then wrap the packets in plastic wrap and refrigerate them for up to one day.

Atomic Artichoke and Parmesan Dip

This is a classic dip that goes back to parties in the 1960s, and it's always a hit and makes you look really sophisticated when you serve it. The combo of the artichoke hearts and cheese laced with loaded mayo is great.

1 cup freshly grated Parmesan cheese
⅔ cup Amazing Mayo (page 16)
½ cup sour cream
2 tablespoons freshly squeezed lemon juice
2 tablespoons chopped fresh parsley
1 tablespoon fresh thyme or 1 teaspoon dried
1 garlic clove, minced
3 scallions, white parts only, trimmed and cut into ½-inch pieces
2 (10-ounce) packages frozen artichoke hearts, thawed and drained
Salt and freshly ground black pepper to taste

YIELD: 8 to 10 servings
ACTIVE TIME: 15 minutes
START TO FINISH: 5 minutes

1. Combine Parmesan, mayonnaise, sour cream, lemon juice, parsley, thyme, and garlic in a 2-quart heavy saucepan. Stir well.

2. Place scallions and artichoke hearts in a food processor fitted with the steel blade. Chop finely using on-and-off pulsing. Scrape mixture into the saucepan, stir well, and season to taste with salt and pepper.

3. Place the saucepan over medium heat and cook, stirring occasionally, for 5 minutes, or until the mixture is bubbly and hot. To serve, transfer dip to a fondue pot or other heated serving dish. Serve hot.

NOTE: The dip can be prepared for heating up to 2 days in advance and refrigerated, tightly covered.

Artichokes are related to thistles and sunflowers, and they were born in the Mediterranean region. Growing in the field you'd swear they were stoned; these long stalks are bending over with the artichokes basically upside down. What we're eating is the plant's flower bud. If allowed to flower, the blossoms measure up to seven inches in diameter and are a beautiful violet-blue color. Artichokes do not pair well with wine because they contain cynarine, an enzyme that causes food eaten immediately after to take on a sweet taste. The cheese in this recipe mitigates that effect.

Boosted Bruschetta

Bruschetta (pronounced brew-SKEH-tah) is just a fancy word for toast that's rubbed with a garlic clove while still hot. As long as you're munching to get the munchies, might as well let the toast be the same as a toke too.

1 thin French baguette
¼ cup Augmented Oil (page 15)
1 large garlic clove, halved lengthwise

YIELD: 18 slices
ACTIVE TIME: 10 minutes
START TO FINISH: 15 minutes

1. Light a charcoal or gas grill, or preheat the oven broiler.
2. Slice bread into ½-inch slices. Brush bread lightly with oil. Grill or broil bread slices for 45 seconds to 1 minute per side, or until toasted. Rub cut side on garlic clove on 1 side of toast.

NOTE: The slices can be toasted up to 2 days in advance and kept at room temperature in an airtight container.

According to Alan Davidson, author of *The Oxford Companion to Food*, bruschetta was invented in Tuscany as a way to show off the benefits of the current year's olive harvest.

So Sweet and So Salty Tapenade

This lusty dip contains both dark olives and dark raisins, so the combination of sweet and salty flavors comes as a surprise, as does the high that follows eating it. All tapenade was born in Provence, but this version is now all-American.

YIELD: 6 to 8 servings
ACTIVE TIME: 10 minutes
START TO FINISH: 10 minutes

1½ cups pitted Kalamata olives
  or other brine-cured black olives
¾ cup raisins
2 garlic cloves, minced
2 tablespoons anchovy paste or ½ teaspoon salt
1 tablespoon chopped fresh parsley
½ teaspoon dried thyme
3 tablespoons freshly squeezed lemon juice
⅔ cup Augmented Oil (page 15)
Freshly ground black pepper to taste

NOTE: The spread can be made up to 2 days in advance and refrigerated, tightly covered. Allow it to reach room temperature before serving.

1. Combine olives, raisins, garlic, anchovy paste, parsley, thyme, and lemon juice in a food processor fitted with the steel blade. Puree until smooth. Add oil slowly through the feed tube, and mix well.

2. Scrape mixture into a mixing bowl, and season to taste with pepper. Serve immediately.

Heat and light are the two worst enemies of dried herbs and spices, so a pretty display rack over the stove is about the worst place to store them. Keep them in a cool, dark place to preserve their potency. The best test for freshness and potency is to smell the contents. If you don't smell a strong aroma, you need a new bottle.

Cha-Cha Chile con Queso

Grab a bowl of tortilla chips and dig in! This hot dip has it all; there are spicy chiles, creamy cheeses, tomatoes, beef, and bong all together. While tortilla chips are best, anything including a spoon will do.

⅓ cup Augmented Oil (page 15)
1 small onion, diced
2 garlic cloves, minced
½ pound lean ground beef
2 ripe plum tomatoes, cored, seeded, and chopped
2 chipotle chiles in adobo sauce, finely chopped
½ cup Bhang Booster (page 17)
1 cup grated Monterey Jack cheese
1 cup grated cheddar cheese
2 teaspoons cornstarch
Freshly ground black pepper to taste

Yield: 6 to 8 servings
Active time: 15 minutes
Start to finish: 30 minutes

1. Heat oil in a large heavy skillet over medium-high heat. Add onion, garlic, and ground beef. Cook, breaking up lumps with a fork, for 3 to 5 minutes, or until brown and no pink remains. Add tomatoes and chipotle chiles, and cook for an additional 3 minutes. Remove the contents of the skillet with a slotted spoon, and discard grease from the skillet.

2. Return mixture to the skillet, and add Bhang Booster, Monterey Jack, and cheddar cheese. Cook the mixture over low heat, stirring frequently, for 3 minutes, or until cheeses melt and are bubbly.

NOTE: The dip can be prepared up to 2 days in advance and refrigerated, tightly covered. Reheat it over low heat, covered, until hot, stirring occasionally.

I don't know about warding off vampires, but the medicinal properties of garlic have scientific backing. It's really good stuff! It is not an accident that garlic is indigenous to central Asia, the area where people live the longest and where the occurrence of cancer is the lowest known. Garlic has also been shown to lower blood pressure and reduce LDL (bad) cholesterol.

Did you know that growing pot had its own tax stamp? Yup. On October 2, 1937, President Roosevelt signed the Marijuana Tax Law. The law made it illegal to possess marijuana in the U.S. without a special tax stamp issued by the U.S. Treasury Department. In theory, growing and selling marijuana was still legal as long as you bought the government tax stamp for $1.00. However, the Treasury Department did not issue any tax stamps for marijuana. There was the original "Catch 22."

Gobs of Garlic Ganga Bean Dip

This is really fast to make, and the flavors will dance in your mouth as the high kicks in. There's some tart lemon, a few herbs, roasted red peppers for color, and loads of garlic for flavor.

2 roasted red bell peppers, peeled, seeded, and diced
2 (15-ounce) cans cannellini beans, drained and rinsed
⅔ cup Augmented Oil (page 15)
¼ cup freshly squeezed lemon juice
5 garlic cloves, minced
½ cup chopped fresh parsley
1 tablespoon fresh thyme or 1 teaspoon dried
Salt and freshly ground black pepper to taste

YIELD: 6 to 8 servings
ACTIVE TIME: 10 minutes
START TO FINISH: 10 minutes

1. Place roasted peppers in the work bowl of a food processor fitted with the steel blade. Chop finely using on-and-off pulsing. Scrape peppers into a mixing bowl.

2. Combine beans, oil, lemon juice, and garlic in a food processor fitted with the steel blade. Puree until smooth. Scrape puree into the mixing bowl, and fold in parsley and thyme. Season to taste with salt and pepper, and serve immediately.

NOTE: The dip can be made up to 2 days in advance and refrigerated, tightly covered. Allow it to reach room temperature before serving.

VARIATIONS:
- Substitute ½ cup sundried tomatoes packed in olive oil, drained, for the red peppers.
- Substitute chopped fresh basil for the parsley and thyme.

Hashish Hummus

Hummus, based on garbanzo beans flavored with sesame, lemon, and garlic, is the onion dip of the twenty-first century. If you've got a few cans of beans in the pantry, you're munching this dip to get the munchies in minutes.

YIELD: 6 to 8 servings
ACTIVE TIME: 10 minutes
START TO FINISH: 10 minutes

2 (15-ounce) cans garbanzo beans, drained with liquid reserved, and rinsed
⅔ cup well-stirred tahini
⅔ cup Augmented Oil (page 15)
3 garlic cloves, minced
⅓ cup freshly squeezed lemon juice, or to taste
Salt and freshly ground black pepper to taste

1. Combine garbanzo beans, tahini, oil, garlic, and lemon juice in a food processor fitted with the steel blade or in a blender. Puree until smooth. Add some reserved bean liquid if too thick. Scrape mixture into a mixing bowl.
2. Season to taste with salt and pepper, and serve immediately.

NOTE: The dip can be made up to 2 days in advance and refrigerated, tightly covered. Allow it to reach room temperature before serving.

VARIATIONS:
- Add up to 3 tablespoons extra lemon juice, plus some lemon zest.
- Add a pureed roasted red bell pepper.
- Add 2 tablespoons horseradish.
- Add up to 3 more garlic cloves, or up to 3 tablespoons roasted garlic.
- Add ½ cup toasted pine nuts as a garnish.
- Add up to 1 teaspoon crushed red pepper flakes or hot red pepper sauce.
- Add 2 tablespoons smoked Spanish paprika.
- Add ½ cup chopped cooked spinach and ¼ cup freshly grated Parmesan cheese.

Acapulco Gold Nocturnal Nachos

Nachos are American, not Mexican, although there are related dishes South of the Border. These are based on some refried beans made with hooch-laced oil to refry your mind too.

⅔ cup Augmented Oil (page 15), divided
1 small onion, chopped
2 garlic cloves, minced
1 to 2 jalapeño or serrano chiles, seeds and ribs removed, and chopped
2 (15-ounce) cans red kidney beans, drained and rinsed
½ cup vegetable stock or chicken stock
Salt and freshly ground black pepper to taste
¼ cup chopped fresh cilantro
1 (12- to 14-ounce) bag restaurant-style tortilla chips
2 cups grated Monterey Jack cheese
6 scallions, white parts and 3 inches of green tops, thinly sliced
2 ripe plum tomatoes, cored, seeded, and chopped
¾ cup sour cream

1. Preheat the oven to 350°F and line a baking sheet with heavy-duty aluminum foil.

2. Heat 2 tablespoons oil in a large skillet over medium-high heat. Add onion, garlic, and chiles, and cook, stirring frequently, for 3 minutes, or until onions are translucent, stirring frequently. Scrape mixture into a food processor fitted with the steel blade.

3. Add beans and stock to the food processor. Process until mixture is pureed but the consistency is still chunky.

4. Heat remaining oil in a deep skillet over medium heat, and add beans. Cook over low heat, stirring constantly, until beans are thick and some of liquid has evaporated, about 10 minutes. Season to taste with salt and pepper, and stir in cilantro.

5. Arrange tortilla chips on the prepared baking sheet, and top with bean mixture. Sprinkle with cheese.

6. Bake for 10 to 12 minutes, or until cheese melts and beans are bubbly. Remove nachos from the oven and top with scallions, tomato, and sour cream. Serve immediately.

NOTE: The beans can be prepared up to 2 days in advance and refrigerated, tightly covered. Add 2 to 3 minutes to the baking time if the beans are chilled.

VARIATIONS:
- Substitute jalapeño Jack for the Monterey Jack for really spicy nachos.
- Top the beans with some shredded cooked chicken.

When you cut open your garlic cloves there might be a green shoot inside. Discard it because it's bitter. While it might not matter if you're just using a clove or two, if you're using a lot it will be unpleasant.

Souped-Up Cereal Mix

While we all know that marijuana is not addictive, this snack mix is. It's the same thing you've eaten all your life, but the buttery goodness in this version comes with a kick.

12 tablespoons Bong Butter (page 14)
3 tablespoons Worcestershire sauce
1 tablespoon Cajun seasoning
2 cups Corn Chex cereal
2 cups Rice Chex cereal
2 cups Wheat Chex cereal
1 cup mixed roasted nuts
1 cup miniature pretzels

YIELD: 6 to 8 servings
ACTIVE TIME: 10 minutes
START TO FINISH: 25 minutes

NOTE: The mix can be stored in an airtight container for up to 1 week. It can also be baked in a 250°F oven for 45 minutes, stirring every 15 minutes.

VARIATIONS:
- Substitute 6 cups of popped popcorn for the cereals.
- Substitute 1 tablespoon hot red pepper sauce for the Worcestershire sauce.

1. Combine butter, Worcestershire, and Cajun seasoning in a microwave-safe cup. Microwave on High (100 percent power) for 30 seconds. Stir, and repeat as needed until butter melts.

2. Combine corn cereal, rice cereal, wheat cereal, nuts, and pretzels in a large glass or plastic mixing bowl. Pour butter mixture over dry ingredients, and stir well to coat evenly.

3. Microwave on High (100 percent power) for 2 minutes. Stir, and repeat. Allow to cool 5 minutes before serving.

Back in the 1950s, when TV was just starting to catch on, there were all sorts of foods and other sociological tie-ins to the telly. TV dinners to eat on small folding TV tables date from 1952, and a mix of greasy crunchies to nibble, called Chex Mix or Chex Party Mix, dates from the same year.

Cheeba Cheese and Salami Torta

This is pretty as hell, with layers of cheese studded with olives and tomatoes alternating with some chopped salami. If you want to make it look fancy, instead of chopping the salami, spread the slices with the cheese and roll them up like little cigars.

1 (8-ounce) packages cream cheese, softened
12 tablespoons Bong Butter (page 14), softened
½ cup chopped pimiento-stuffed green olives
¼ cup chopped sun-dried tomatoes
3 scallions, white parts and 3 inches of green tops, chopped
2 garlic cloves, minced
2 teaspoons Italian seasoning
Salt and crushed red pepper flakes to taste
⅓ pound Genoa salami, chopped

YIELD: 6 to 8 servings
ACTIVE TIME: 15 minutes
START TO FINISH: 1 hour, including 45 minutes for chilling

NOTE: The torta can be prepared up to 2 days in advance and refrigerated, tightly covered with plastic wrap. Allow it to sit at room temperature for 30 minutes before serving.

1. Combine cream cheese and butter in a mixing bowl, and beat at medium speed with an electric mixer until light and fluffy. Stir in olives, sun-dried tomatoes, scallions, garlic, and Italian seasoning, and mix well. Season to taste with salt and red pepper flakes and mix well again.

2. Line a small mixing bowl with plastic wrap. Place one-third of cheese mixture in the mixing bowl, and smooth the top. Layer with one-half of salami, and then layer cheese, salami, and finally cheese. Chill torta for 45 minutes.

3. To serve, invert torta onto a platter, and remove plastic wrap. Serve with slices of Boosted Bruschetta (page 22) or crackers or slices of bread.

The easiest way to soften cream cheese is in the microwave. Remove the cream cheese from the foil wrapper, cut it into 1 tablespoon amounts, and microwave it at 20 percent power for 20 seconds. Repeat, if necessary.

Canappa Cheddar Crackers

Admittedly, reading crushed potato chips in the ingredient list is unusual, but they make these the crunchiest as well as most flavorful cheese crackers you'll ever taste. These might be the ultimate head snack.

1 (5.5-ounce) bag potato chips
6 ounces (1 ½ cups) grated sharp cheddar cheese
8 tablespoons Bong Butter (page 14), melted
⅓ cup all-purpose flour
½ teaspoon cayenne, or to taste

YIELD: 6 to 8 servings
ACTIVE TIME: 10 minutes
START TO FINISH: 30 minutes

1. Preheat the oven to 350°F. Place potato chips in a food processor fitted with a steel blade. Coarsely chop chips, using on-and-off pulsing. This can also be done by placing chips in a heavy resealable plastic bag, and hitting chips with the bottom of a heavy skillet.

2. Scrape potato chip crumbs into a mixing bowl, and add cheese, butter, flour, and cayenne. Stir until mixture is combined and holds together when pressed in the palm of your hand.

3. Form 1 tablespoon of mixture into a ball. Place it on an ungreased baking sheet and flatten it into a circle with the bottom of a floured glass or with your fingers. Repeat with remaining dough, leaving 1 inch between circles.

4. Bake for 15 to 18 minutes, or until browned. Cool crackers on the baking sheet for 2 minutes, then transfer to a cooling rack with a spatula to cool completely. Serve at room temperature.

NOTE: The crackers can be made 2 days in advance and kept at room temperature in an airtight container.

VARIATIONS:
- Substitute jalapeño Jack for the cheddar cheese, and substitute crushed corn chips for the potato chips.
- Substitute a flavored potato chip, like barbecue or sour cream and onion, for the plain chips.

Pot-Filled Potato Puffs

These easy and cheesy puffs containing lots of stuff you can also puff are like miniature versions of stuffed baked potatoes. There's Swiss cheese and potato together, and they get a crunchy crust when they're baked.

½ pound russet potatoes, peeled and cut into 1-inch dice
⅔ cup all-purpose flour
8 tablespoons Bong Butter (page 14), softened and cut into small pieces
1 large egg, lightly beaten
4 ounces (1 cup) grated Swiss cheese
½ teaspoon salt or to taste
Cayenne to taste

YIELD: 4 to 6 servings
ACTIVE TIME: 15 minutes
START TO FINISH: 40 minutes

NOTE: The puffs can be prepared up to 2 days in advance and refrigerated, tightly covered. Reheat them in a 375°F oven for 3 to 5 minutes, or until hot. Undercook sticks slightly if you're planning on reheating them.

The ancient Incas first started cultivating potatoes thousands of years ago, and the first conquistadors exported the tubers to Europe. Potatoes were not popular, however, until Sir Walter Raleigh planted them on his estate in Ireland in the eighteenth century.

1. Preheat the oven to 425°F, and grease two baking sheets or line them with silicon baking mats.

2. Boil potatoes in salted water for 10 to 12 minutes, or until very tender when pierced with a knife. Drain potatoes, shaking the colander vigorously to extract as much liquid as possible. Return potatoes to the pan, and mash well or put potatoes through a ricer.

3. Cook mashed potatoes over low heat for 1 to 2 minutes, or until they begin to form a film on the bottom of the pan. Beat in flour, then butter, bit by bit, beating well to ensure that butter melts; place the pan over low heat if butter is not melting in. Beat in egg, cheese, and salt, and season to taste with cayenne.

4. Drop the mixture by scant tablespoons onto the baking sheets, and flatten the mounds to ½-inch. Bake for 10 to 12 minutes, or until browned. Serve hot.

YIELD: 6 to 8 servings
ACTIVE TIME: 15 minutes
START TO FINISH: 45 minutes

Cheesy Cannabis Puffs

There's a fancy dish served in France called Gougères; they're like baby cream puffs with cheese in the batter. Well, here they are without the fancy name so you don't have to worry about how to pronounce these crusty puffs when you serve them to friends.

1 cup chicken stock
6 tablespoons Bong Butter (page 14)
½ teaspoon salt
¼ teaspoon freshly grated nutmeg
Pinch of freshly grated white pepper
1 cup all-purpose flour
4 large eggs
1 cup grated Gruyère cheese

1. Preheat the oven to 400º F, and line two baking sheets with parchment paper or silicon baking mats.

2. Combine stock, butter, salt, nutmeg, and pepper in a small saucepan, and bring to a boil over medium-high heat, stirring occasionally. Remove the pan from the heat, and add flour all

at once. Using a wooden paddle or wide wooden spoon, beat flour into the liquid until smooth. Then place the saucepan over high heat and beat mixture constantly for 1 to 2 minutes, until it forms a mass that leaves the sides of the pan and begins to film the bottom of the pot.

3. Transfer mixture to a food processor fitted with the steel blade. Add eggs, 1 at a time, beating well between each addition and scraping the sides of the work bowl between each addition. Then add cheese, and mix well again.

4. Using a soup spoon dipped in cold water, form dough into mounds 1 inch in diameter and ½ inch high onto the baking sheets, allowing 2 inches between puffs.

5. Bake puffs for 20 to 25 minutes, or until puffs are golden brown and crusty to the touch. Remove the pans from the oven, and using the tip of a paring knife, cut a slit in the side of each puff to allow the steam to escape. Turn off the oven, and place baked puffs back into the oven with the oven door ajar for 10 minutes to finish crisping. Remove puffs from the oven, and serve immediately.

NOTE: The puffs can be made up to 2 days in advance and refrigerated, tightly covered; they can also be frozen for up to 2 weeks. Reheat chilled puffs in a 350°F oven for 10 minutes and frozen puffs for 15 minutes.

Did you know you could get a high from nutmeg? Probably not the tiny amount in these puffs or the sprinkle on a glass of eggnog at Christmas, but this spice has hallucinogenic properties. Who knew? The problem is that you usually get nauseous before you get high, so stick to stash. But if your cupboard is barren, there's always the spice pantry to explore.

Yerba Buena Parmesan Crisps

These look like cookies when you put them out, and they're just as crispy as a good butter cookie because they've got lots of Bong Butter along with cheese and herbs in the dough.

1 cup (16 tablespoons) Bong Butter (page 14), softened

1 large egg yolk

7 tablespoons heavy cream, divided

1 tablespoon granulated sugar

2 teaspoons Italian seasoning, or some combination of dried oregano, basil, thyme, and rosemary

1 teaspoon salt

Freshly ground black pepper to taste

1¾ cups all-purpose flour

1 cup freshly grated Parmesan cheese

1 large egg

YIELD: 8 to 10 servings
ACTIVE TIME: 15 minutes
START TO FINISH: 40 minutes

NOTE: The crisps can be made up to 2 weeks in advance and kept at room temperature in an airtight container.

1. Preheat the oven to 325°F, and grease two baking sheets or cover them with silicon baking mats.

2. Combine butter, egg yolk, 6 tablespoons cream, sugar, Italian seasoning, salt, and pepper in a mixing bowl, and beat at medium speed with an electric mixer for 2 minutes, or until light and fluffy. Beat in flour and cheese at low speed.

3. Form mixture into 1 tablespoon balls, and place them 2 inches apart on the prepared baking sheets. Flatten balls with the bottom or a glass dipped in flour.

4. Beat egg with remaining 1 tablespoon cream, and paint tops of cookies with mixture using a pastry brush or your finger.

5. Bake for 20 to 25 minutes, rotating pans halfway through, or until golden. Cool crisps briefly on the baking sheets, and then transfer to wire cooling racks to cool completely.

YIELD: 4 to 6 servings
ACTIVE TIME: 10 minutes
START TO FINISH: 12 minutes

Hooched Herb and Garlic Bread

Once you've gotten into the habit of keeping Bong Butter in the refrigerator you'll find all sorts of ways to use it. This variation on garlic bread is one of the fastest and easiest. Plus it's really tasty!

8 tablespoons Bong Butter (page 14), melted
¼ cup Augmented Oil (page 15)
3 tablespoons chopped fresh parsley
2 scallions, white parts and 4 inches of green tops,
  finely chopped
4 to 6 garlic cloves, pressed through a garlic press
1 teaspoon Italian seasoning
Salt and freshly ground black pepper to taste
1 (¾-pound) loaf Italian bread or ciabatta
¼ cup freshly grated Parmesan cheese

NOTE: The butter mixture can be prepared up to 4 hours in advance and kept at room temperature.

VARIATION:
- Substitute cilantro for the parsley, and substitute 1 tablespoon of chili powder for the Italian seasoning.

1. Preheat the oven broiler, and line a broiler pan with heavy-duty aluminum foil.

2. Combine butter, oil, parsley, scallions, garlic, Italian seasoning, salt, and pepper in a mixing bowl. Cut bread in half horizontally, and separate the halves. Place halves cut-side down on the pan, and broil for 1 minute.

3. Turn bread over and brush garlic mixture all over cuts sides of bread. Sprinkle Parmesan on top of butter mixture. Broil for 1½ to 2 minutes, or until golden brown. Serve immediately.

YIELD: **4 to 6 servings**
ACTIVE TIME: **25 minutes**
START TO FINISH: **35 minutes**

Outrageous Onion Pizza Niçoise (Pissaladière)

Those French folk use so much oil and butter in their cooking
that their snacks are naturals to make with marijuana.
This pizza has sweet caramelized onions on top of a garlicky
green topping.

4 tablespoons Bong Butter (page 14)
½ cup Augmented Oil (page 15), divided
4 large sweet onions such as Bermuda or Vidalia, peeled and thinly sliced
2 teaspoons granulated sugar
½ teaspoon salt or to taste
Freshly ground black pepper to taste
½ cup chopped fresh parsley
½ cup Italian breadcrumbs
4 tablespoons anchovy paste
3 garlic cloves, minced
1 large egg yolk
1 tablespoon balsamic vinegar
1 tablespoon freshly squeezed lemon juice
1 (12-inch) ready-to-bake pizza crust, such as Boboli
½ cup chopped oil-cured black olives
4 anchovy fillets, thinly sliced (optional)

1. Preheat the oven to 450ºF, and place a baking stone or baking sheet in the oven to preheat.

2. Melt butter and 2 tablespoons oil in a large skillet over medium heat. Add onions, sugar, salt, and pepper, and toss to coat onions. Cover the skillet, and cook for 10 minutes, stirring occasionally. Uncover the skillet, and cook over medium-high heat for 15 to 20 minutes, or until onions are browned. Stir frequently toward the end of the cooking time, and stir any browned juices on the skillet into the onions.

3. While onions cook, combine parsley, breadcrumbs, anchovy paste, garlic, egg yolk, vinegar, and lemon juice in a food processor fitted with the steel blade or in a blender. Puree until smooth. Slowly add remaining oil, and continue to process until smooth and thick.

4. Spread pizza crust with mixture, stopping 1 inch from the edge. Arrange onions on top of sauce, and sprinkle with olives, and anchovy slivers, if using.

5. Bake pizza on pizza stone or baking sheet for 8 to 10 minutes. Cut pizza into small squares, and serve hot.

NOTE: The onions and parsley mixtures can be prepared up to 2 days in advance and refrigerated, tightly covered.

The most time-consuming part of this dish is caramelizing the onions, and there's no reason you couldn't do a double or triple batch and freeze what's not needed for this recipe. With the leftovers, future onion soup or any number of dishes are just moments away from completion.

Spicy Spiked Cornmeal Muffins

These are muffins that don't belong on the breakfast table! They're laced with cayenne and spicy jalapeño Jack cheese, and they're a great snack.

1 cup all-purpose flour
1 cup yellow cornmeal
1 tablespoon baking powder
1 tablespoon granulated sugar
1 teaspoon ground cumin
½ teaspoon salt
½ teaspoon baking soda
½ teaspoon cayenne
1 cup buttermilk, shaken well
⅔ cup Augmented Oil (page 15)
1 large egg
1 cup grated jalapeño Jack cheese, divided

YIELD: 12 muffins
ACTIVE TIME: 10 minutes
START TO FINISH: 30 minutes

1. Preheat the oven to 400°F, and grease a 12-cup muffin pan; you can also use paper liners.

2. Combine flour, cornmeal, baking powder, sugar, cumin, salt, baking soda, and cayenne in a large mixing bowl, and whisk well. Add buttermilk, oil, egg, and 2/3 cup cheese. Stir gently to wet flour, but do not whisk until smooth; batter should be lumpy. Fill each prepared cup 2/3 full, and sprinkle with remaining cheese.

3. Bake muffins for 18 to 20 minutes, or until a toothpick inserted in the center comes out clean. Place muffin pan on a cooling rack for 10 minutes, then serve.

NOTE: Muffins can be served hot or at room temperature.

VARIATIONS:
- Substitute cheddar cheese for the jalapeño Jack, and omit the cumin and cayenne.
- Add 1 tablespoon Italian seasoning and 1 garlic clove, peeled and pushed through a garlic press, to batter.

Cleaning a grater once you've grated cheese can be a bitch. The same is true for the grating disk of a food processor. To make the cheese come off more easily, spray the grater or grating disk with vegetable oil spray before you start grating.

Maybe the late William F. Buckley, Jr. was conservative when it came to politics, but not to pot. He wrote: "Even if one takes every reefer madness allegation of the prohibitionists at face value, marijuana prohibition has done far more harm to far more people than marijuana ever could."

YIELD: 8 to 12 servings
ACTIVE TIME: 20 minutes
START TO FINISH: 3½ hour

F**ked Up Focaccia

There's something so, so tactile about bread dough, especially if you're stoned. Italian focaccia, pronounced foe-KAH-cha, is one of the world's great nibble foods, as well as being flat so it's perfect for splitting into a sandwich.

3 (¼-ounce) packages active dry yeast
2¼ cups warm water (110°to 115°F)
1 tablespoon granulated sugar
1 teaspoon salt
7 cups all-purpose flour, plus additional if necessary, divided
⅔ cup Augmented Oil (page 15), divided
Kosher salt and freshly ground black for sprinkling

1. Combine yeast, water, sugar, salt, and ¼ cup flour in a mixing bowl, and whisk well to dissolve yeast. Set aside for 5 minutes, or until mixture begins to become foamy.

2. Transfer mixture to the bowl of a standard electric mixer fitted with the paddle attachment. Add ⅓ cup oil and remaining flour, and beat a low speed until flour is incorporated to form a soft dough.

3. Place the dough hook on the mixer, and knead dough at medium speed for 2 minutes. Raise the speed to high, and knead for an additional 3 to 4 minutes, or until dough forms a soft ball and is springy. If kneading by hand, it will take about 10 to 12 minutes. Oil a mixing bowl, and add dough, turning it to make sure the top is oiled. Cover the bowl with a sheet of plastic wrap, and place it in a warm spot for 1 to 2 hours, or until dough doubles in bulk.

4. Preheat the oven to 450°F, and oil an 11 x 17-inch baking sheet. Gently press dough into the prepared pan; allow dough to rest 5 minutes if it is difficult to work with. Cover the pan with a sheet of oiled plastic wrap, and let rise in a warm place until doubled in bulk, about 30 minutes.

5. Make indentations in dough at 1-inch intervals with oiled fingertips. Drizzle with remaining oil, and sprinkle with kosher salt and pepper. Bake in lower third of oven until deep golden on top and pale golden on bottom, 25 to 30 minutes. Transfer bread to a rack and serve warm or at room temperature.

NOTE: This amount of dough is about the maximum that a home standard mixer can make, so the recipe cannot be increased. However, it can be made smaller proportionally.

VARIATIONS:
- Sprinkle the top with ¼ cup of a chopped fresh herb such as rosemary, basil, or oregano, or some combination.
- Spread sautéed onions or fennel across the top of the dough before baking.
- Soak four garlic cloves, peeled and minced, in the oil for 2 hours before making the dough. Either strain and discard garlic, or use it if you really like things garlicky.

chapter 3

MAIN MEAL MUNCHIES

Even though the title of this book is *Stoner Snacks*, including some recipes for dynamite dinners that can be on the table really fast seemed like a good idea. There are a lot of pastas in this chapter, so even if all you have to cook on is a hotplate in your dorm room you can still cook your way to giggle smoke greatness.

Many of the recipes are vegetarian. If you're having friends over for some "fu food" you can't go wrong with a vegetarian dish; everyone eats them. It's when you start with meats that most people have problems. But chicken is the meat that's most popular today, and it's cheap so you're not breaking the boom bank to buy it. It also takes to a kaleidoscope of seasonings, as you'll see here.

I suggest serving a tossed salad with many of these dishes, and if you make your own salad dressing be sure to sub some Augmented Oil (page 15) for basic olive oil. Adding some ganga to your greens is a great treat.

Panzanella with Punch

This Tuscan bread and tomato salad, with some crunchy healthful vegetables thrown in, is the epitome of emotional satisfaction.

1 (½-pound) loaf Italian or French bread
2 cups very hot tap water
½ cup red wine vinegar, divided
Freshly ground black pepper to taste
3 large ripe tomatoes, cored, seeded, and diced, divided
3 garlic cloves, minced
1 tablespoon anchovy paste or ½ teaspoon salt
⅔ cup Augmented Oil (page 15)
½ small red onion, diced
1 cucumber, peeled, halved lengthwise, seeded, and diced
½ cup firmly packed shredded fresh basil
2 tablespoons chopped fresh parsley
2 tablespoons capers, rinsed

YIELD: **4 to 6 servings**
ACTIVE TIME: **20 minutes**
START TO FINISH: **1½ hours, including 1 hour to soak bread**

NOTE: The salad can be prepared up to 1 day in advance and refrigerated, tightly covered.

VARIATION:
- Got some leftover chicken in the refrigerator? Throw up to 2 cups of it in.

1. Cut or tear bread into 1½-inch cubes, and place it in a mixing bowl. Stir water and ¼ cup vinegar together, and pour over bread cubes. Stir cubes to moisten evenly, and sprinkle with salt and pepper. Set aside for 1 hour at room temperature. Drain bread, if necessary, and return it to the mixing bowl.

2. While bread soaks, combine remaining vinegar, ⅓ of tomato, garlic, anchovy paste, and pepper in a food processor fitted with the steel blade or in a blender. Puree until smooth. Add oil, and mix well. Set aside. Place remaining tomatoes on a plate, and season to taste with salt and pepper.

3. Add tomatoes, onion, cucumber, basil, parsley, and capers to the mixing bowl with bread, and toss with dressing.

Blue Sage Spiked Pasta Salad
with Tomatoes and White Beans

This cold pasta salad is simultaneously hearty and refreshing. The garlic and sage add savory flavor to the pasta and beans, and the special oil in your dressing makes you realize how great cold pasta can be.

¾ pound small shells
⅔ cup Augmented Oil (page 15)
4 garlic cloves, minced
2 tablespoons dried sage
4 ripe plum tomatoes, cored, seeded, and chopped
1 (15-ounce) can cannellini beans, drained and rinsed
Salt and freshly ground black pepper to taste
½ cup freshly grated Parmesan cheese (optional)

YIELD: 4 to 6 servings
ACTIVE TIME: 15 minutes
START TO FINISH: 30 minute

1. Bring a large pot of salted water to a boil. Add pasta, and cook according to package directions until al dente. Drain pasta, and rinse under cold running water until pasta is cool. Drain, and refrigerate.

2. While water is heating, heat oil in a large skillet over medium-high heat. Add garlic and sage, and cook, stirring constantly, for 1 minute. Scrape mixture into a large mixing bowl, and add tomatoes and beans.

NOTE: The salad can be prepared up to 1 day in advance and refrigerated, tightly covered.

3. Add pasta to mixing bowl, season with salt and pepper, and serve at room temperature or chilled. Toss with Parmesan cheese just prior to serving, if using.

Running pasta under cold water after draining speeds up the completion of all pasta salads.

Green Goddess Radiatore with Roasted Vegetables and Olives

Roasting caramelizes the natural sugars in vegetables and evaporates their water. This is a simple sauce with an intense and hearty flavor. Serve it with a tossed salad.

⅔ pound radiatore
1 (1-pound) eggplant, cut into 3/4-inch dice
1 large onion, diced
8 ripe plum tomatoes, cored, seeded, and diced
⅔ cup Augmented Oil (page 15)
4 garlic cloves, minced
Salt and freshly ground black pepper to taste
½ cup chopped pitted kalamata olives
½ cup freshly grated Parmesan cheese

YIELD: 4 to 6 servings
ACTIVE TIME: 15 minutes
START TO FINISH: 40 minutes

NOTE: The vegetable mixture can be made 1 day in advance and refrigerated, tightly covered. Reheat it, covered, in a 350°F oven for 10 to 12 minutes, or until hot.

1. Preheat the oven to 450°F, and line a rimmed baking sheet with heavy-duty aluminum foil. Bring a large pot of salted water to a boil. Add pasta, and cook according to package directions until al dente. Drain, reserving 1 cup of pasta water, and return pasta to the pot.

2. While water heats, combine eggplant, onion, and tomatoes on the prepared pan. Add oil and garlic, and mix well to coat vegetables. Season to taste with salt and pepper, and roast vegetables for 20 to 25 minutes, or until tender. Stir vegetables after 10 minutes.

3. Add roasted eggplant mixture, olives, and Parmesan to the pot with pasta. Toss to coat, adding ¼ to ½ cup pasta water, if mixture seems dry. Serve immediately.

Linguine in Creamy Cannabis Tomato Sauce

In the past couple of years spiking creamy tomato sauces with vodka has become the rage. But this one has weed in multiple forms. Sure beats a shot of vodka any day. The sauce contains some veggies and herbs, which boost the flavor along with the bamba.

¾ pound linguine
3 tablespoons Augmented Oil (page 15)
1 large onion, diced
2 celery ribs, chopped
3 garlic cloves, minced
1 ½ teaspoons dried oregano
1 teaspoon dried thyme
1 (8-ounce) can tomato sauce
1 (14.5-ounce) can diced tomatoes, undrained
1 cup Bhang Booster (page 17)
3 tablespoons Bong Butter (page 14)
2 tablespoons chopped fresh parsley
Salt and freshly ground black pepper to taste
½ cup freshly grated Parmesan cheese

YIELD: 4 to 6 servings
ACTIVE TIME: 15 minutes
START TO FINISH: 35 minutes

1. Bring a large pot of salted water to a boil. Add pasta, and cook according to package directions until al dente. Drain, and set aside.

2. While water heats, heat oil in a saucepan over medium-high heat. Add onion, celery, and garlic, and cook, stirring frequently, for 3 minutes, or until onion is translucent. Add oregano and thyme, and cook for 1 minute, stirring constantly. Stir in tomato sauce, tomatoes, Bhang Booster, butter, and parsley.

3. Bring sauce to a boil, reduce the heat to low, and simmer, uncovered, stirring occasionally, for 20 minutes. Add pasta to sauce, season to taste with salt and pepper, and serve immediately, passing Parmesan cheese separately.

NOTE: The sauce can be prepared up to 3 days in advance and refrigerated, tightly covered. Reheat over low heat, stirring occasionally, until simmering. Cook pasta just prior to serving.

The flavor of most dried herbs and spices is released if the spices are sautéed with vegetables over low heat before adding them to a liquid.

Pasta with Jolly Green Garlic and Oil (Pasta Aglio e Olio)

Getting a delicious dinner on the table doesn't get any easier than this recipe! As long as you cook with garlic, you've probably got everything you need right in the kitchen, so as soon as the pasta is cooked you're ready to eat, and start feeling really mellow soon after.

¾ pound spaghetti or linguine
⅔ cup Augmented Oil (page 15)
8 garlic cloves, minced
¾ to 1 teaspoon crushed red pepper flakes
Salt to taste
½ cup freshly grated Parmesan cheese

YIELD: 4 to 6 servings
ACTIVE TIME: 10 minutes
START TO FINISH: 25 minutes

1. Bring a large pot of salted water to a boil. Add pasta, and cook according to package directions until al dente. Drain, reserving 1 cup of cooking liquid, and set aside.

2. While pasta cooks, heat oil in a large skillet over medium-high heat. Add garlic and red pepper flakes. Reduce heat to low, and cook, stirring constantly, for 1 minute, or until garlic is golden brown.

3. Remove the pan from the heat, and add the pasta. Toss well, adding some reserved cooking liquid if mixture seems dry. Season to taste with salt, and serve immediately, passing Parmesan cheese separately.

NOTE: The shrimp can be prepared for cooking up to 6 hours in advance and refrigerated, tightly covered.

Shrimp Scampi with Swag

While scampo is the Italian word for prawn, scampi became the term used for any Italian fish preparation that includes butter and wine. Serve this easy dish with a tossed salad and some Hooched Herb and Garlic Bread (page 37) for an even bigger buzz.

1½ pounds raw shrimp, peeled and deveined
6 tablespoons Bong Butter (page 14)
2 tablespoons Augmented Oil (page 15)
4 garlic cloves, minced
1 shallot, chopped
½ cup dry white wine
¼ cup chopped fresh parsley
1 teaspoon Italian seasoning
Salt and crushed red pepper flakes to taste

While butter gives food a delicious flavor it should never be used alone when sautéing food. All fats burn at a certain temperature, and the dairy solids in butter make that temperature rather low. That's why in recipes there is always some sort of oil added to raise the smoke point.

1. Rinse shrimp and pat dry with paper towels.

2. Heat butter and oil in a large skillet over medium-high heat. When butter foam starts to subside, add garlic, shallot, and shrimp. Cook, stirring frequently, for 3 minutes, or until onion is translucent.

3. Add wine, parsley, and Italian seasoning to the skillet. Stir well, and season to taste with salt and red pepper flakes. Cook for 2 minutes. Serve immediately.

Magic Mushroom Quesadillas

These quesadillas have a subtle flavor, with aromatic smoked Spanish paprika giving them great appeal both in terms of taste and color. Serve them with a tossed salad.

4 to 6 (10-inch) flour or
  whole-wheat tortillas

4 tablespoons Bong Butter (page 14)

3 tablespoons Augmented Oil (page 15)

2 garlic cloves, minced

2 tablespoons smoked Spanish paprika

1 teaspoon ground cumin

1 teaspoon dried oregano

¾ pound mushrooms, wiped with a
  damp paper towel,
  trimmed, and thinly sliced

1 cup canned black beans, drained
  and rinsed

Salt and freshly ground black
  pepper to taste

2 cups grated Monterey Jack cheese

Vegetable oil spray

YIELD: 4 to 6 servings
ACTIVE TIME: 15 minutes
START TO FINISH: 30 minutes

1. Preheat the oven to 450°F, cover two baking sheets with heavy-duty aluminum foil, and grease the foil with vegetable oil spray. Soften tortillas, if necessary, by wrapping them in plastic wrap and heating them in a microwave oven on High (100 percent power) for 10 to 15 seconds, or until pliable. Set aside.

2. Heat butter and oil in a large skillet over medium-high heat. Add garlic, paprika, cumin, and oregano, and cook for 30 seconds, stirring constantly. Add mushrooms, and cook for 5 to 7 minutes, or until mushrooms soften. Stir in beans, and season to taste with salt and pepper, and spread evenly on half of each tortilla. Top mushrooms with cheese.

3. Fold blank side of tortillas over filling, and press closed with the palm of your hand or a spatula. Arrange tortillas on prepared baking sheets, and spray tops with vegetable oil spray.

4. Bake quesadillas for 5 minutes. Turn them gently with a spatula, and press them down if the top separates from the filling. Bake for an additional 5 to 7 minutes, or until crispy. Allow to sit for 2 minutes, then cut each in half, and serve immediately.

NOTE: The quesadillas can be formed up to 1 day in advance and refrigerated, tightly covered. Add 3 minutes to the baking time if chilled.

VARIATION:
• Substitute jalapeño Jack for the Monterey Jack for a spicier filling.

While it is the special fats that give these quesadillas their magical properties, be on the lookout for Magic Mushrooms if you're in Mexico or Central America. They contain psilocybin, which is a hallucinogenic that can give you quite the trip.

Twisted Tabbouleh with Shrimp and Feta

This refreshing salad combines tart lemon, aromatic herbs, and crunchy vegetables with a nutty grain. You can make it into "tacos" by rolling it in lettuce leaves. Tabbouleh, pronounced ta-BOOL-a, is a great dish to keep around when you're stoned because it brings in so many of the senses.

¾ pound bulgur wheat
½ cup freshly squeezed lemon juice
2⅓ cups very hot tap water
⅔ cup Augmented Oil (page 15), divided
1 pound raw shrimp, peeled and deveined
Salt and freshly ground black pepper to taste
1 cucumber, seeded, and chopped
4 ripe plum tomatoes, cored, seeded, and chopped
1 small red onion, minced
2 garlic cloves, minced
1 cup chopped fresh parsley
¼ cup chopped fresh mint (optional)
½ cup crumbled feta cheese

YIELD: 4 to 6 servings
ACTIVE TIME: 15 minutes
START TO FINISH: 45 minutes, including 15 minutes to chill

1. Preheat the oven to 400ºF, and line a baking sheet with aluminum foil. Place bulgur in a large mixing bowl and add lemon juice and hot water. Let stand, covered, for 30 minutes, or until bulgur is tender. Drain off any excess liquid.

NOTE: The tabbouleh can be made up to 1 day in advance and refrigerated, tightly covered.

VARIATIONS:
- Substitute boneless, skinless chicken breasts for the shrimp. Cut the chicken into ¾-inch cubes, and bake them for 10 to 12 minutes, or until the chicken is cooked through and no longer pink.
- Omit the shrimp, and increase the feta to 1¼ cups.

2. While bulgur soaks, rinse shrimp and pat dry with paper towels. Rub shrimp with 2 tablespoons oil, and sprinkle with salt and pepper. Bake shrimp for 6 to 8 minutes, or until pink. Set aside.

3. Add shrimp, cucumbers, tomatoes, onion, garlic, parsley, mint, if using, and feta to bulgur and toss to combine. Add remaining oil, and season to taste with salt and pepper.

4. Refrigerate tabbouleh for at least 15 minutes. Serve cold or at room temperature.

> **Tabbouleh hails from Lebanon.** *Guiness World Records* lists a batch of more than 7,800 pounds made in Beruit in 2009 as the record. But to the happy folk of Bristow, Oklahoma, tabbouleh is also a source of pride. Middle Eastern settlers brought it there in the late nineteenth century. There's a festival on the second Saturday of May each year at which Miss Tabbouleh is crowned at the rodeo.

Yerba Buena Chicken Salad

There's a lot to make you happy in this light and easy dish, starting with some high-test oil in the dressing. The combo of chicken with chick peas, olives, and tomatoes is as sunny as a day on the beach in Provence.

1 pound boneless, skinless chicken breast halves
⅔ cup Augmented Oil (page 15), divided
Salt and freshly ground black pepper to taste
2 tablespoons smoked Spanish paprika
1 tablespoon ground cumin
1 tablespoon dried oregano
3 tablespoons balsamic vinegar
3 tablespoons freshly squeezed orange juice
2 tablespoons chopped fresh parsley
2 garlic cloves, minced
1 (15-ounce) can garbanzo beans, drained and rinsed
4 ripe plum tomatoes, cored, seeded, and diced
¼ cup pitted kalamata olives
4 to 6 cups bite-size pieces romaine lettuce, rinsed and dried

YIELD: 4 to 6 servings
ACTIVE TIME: 20 minutes
START TO FINISH: 20 minutes

56

1. Preheat the oven broiler or an electric double-sided grill pan.

2. Rinse chicken and pat dry with paper towels. Trim chicken of all visible fat and pound to an even thickness of ½ inch between two sheets of plastic wrap. Rub chicken with 2 tablespoons oil, and sprinkle with salt and pepper. Combine paprika, cumin, and oregano in a small cup. Rub mixture on both sides of chicken. Cook chicken for 3 to 4 minutes per side, if not using a double-sided grill pan, or until chicken is cooked through and no longer pink. Set chicken aside.

3. While chicken cooks, combine vinegar, orange juice, parsley, garlic, salt, and pepper in a jar with a tight-fitting lid, and shake well. Add remaining oil, and shake well again.

4. Place beans, tomatoes, and olives in a mixing bowl, and add ½ of dressing. Stir well.

5. To serve, arrange lettuce on individual plates or onto a large serving platter, and top with bean mixture. Slice chicken into 2-inch strips, and place on top of vegetables. Drizzle salad greens with remaining dressing, and serve immediately.

NOTE: The chicken can also be cooked up to 1 day in advance and refrigerated, tightly covered, and the dressing can be prepared at the same time. Serve the chicken cold; do not reheat.

VARIATION:
- Substitute boneless pork loin, cut into ¼-inch slices, for the chicken. Cook the pork for 2 to 3 minutes per side.

Balsamic vinegar is traditionally made from white Trebbiano grapes grown in the Modena region of Italy. It gets its rich, dark color and mellow flavor from being aged for many years in wooden barrels, similar to aging a wine.

Cheeba Chicken with Rosemary Butter Sauce

Classic French cooking includes a whole category of sauces called compound butters; all they are is unsalted butter flavored in different ways. This is a fast and refreshing dish, with some tangy lemon juice added to balance the richness of the other flavors.

1½ pounds boneless, skinless chicken thighs or chicken breasts

3 tablespoons all-purpose flour

Salt and freshly ground black pepper to taste

⅓ cup Augmented Oil (page 15)

4 garlic cloves, minced

3 tablespoons chopped fresh rosemary or 1 table-spoon dried

5 tablespoons Bong Butter (page 14)

2 tablespoons freshly squeezed lemon juice

YIELD: 4 to 6 servings
ACTIVE TIME: 20 minutes
START TO FINISH: 20 minutes

NOTE: The dish can be prepared for cooking up to 6 hours in advance, and refrigerated, tightly covered.

VARIATION:
- Substitute cubes of thick firm-fleshed white fish fillets, cut into 1-inch cubes, for the chicken.

1. Rinse chicken and pat dry with paper towels. Trim chicken of all visible fat. Cut chicken into ¾-inch cubes. Toss chicken with flour, salt, and pepper in a bowl. Heat oil in a large skillet over high heat, add chicken cubes, and cook, stirring frequently, for 4 to 5 minutes, or until chicken is cooked through and no longer pink.

2. Add garlic, rosemary, and butter to the skillet and cook for 1 minute, shaking the skillet occasionally to coat chicken. Add lemon juice, and season to taste with salt and pepper. Serve immediately.

Coating food with flour before browning it accomplishes a number of purposes. On one hand, it creates a thin brown skin, and the frying cooks the flour particles. The finished sauce is also lightly thickened from the flour, but with no lingering "flour-y" taste.

Garlicky Spanish Crazy Weed Chicken

It doesn't get much easier than this recipe. There are just a few ingredients and it's on the table in a matter of minutes. I usually serve it with a loaf of crusty bread, along with a tossed salad, to enjoy every drop of the garlicky sauce.

1½ pounds boneless, skinless chicken breast halves
⅔ cup Augmented Oil (page 15)
8 garlic cloves, minced
3 tablespoons smoked Spanish paprika
3 tablespoons chopped fresh parsley
Salt and crushed red pepper flakes to taste

YIELD: 4 to 6 servings
ACTIVE TIME: 10 minutes
START TO FINISH: 20 minutes

1. Rinse chicken and pat dry with paper towels. Trim chicken of all visible fat, and cut into ¾-inch cubes.

2. Heat oil in a large skillet over medium-high heat. Add garlic and paprika, and cook for 1 minute, stirring constantly. Add chicken and parsley, and cook, stirring constantly, for 3 to 4 minutes, or until chicken is cooked through and no longer pink. Season to taste with salt and red pepper flakes, and serve immediately.

NOTE: The chicken can be prepared up to 3 hours in advance and served at room temperature.

VARIATION:
- Substitute thick white-fleshed fish fillets, cut into ¾-inch cubes, for the chicken. Cook for 2 to 3 minutes, or until fish is opaque and flakes easily.

Willie Nelson is quoted as saying, "I think people need to be educated to the fact that marijuana is not a drug. Marijuana is an herb and a flower. God put it here. If He put it here and He wants it to grow, what gives the government the right to say that God is wrong?"

Lobo Lemon Chicken

This is an Italian classic, with chicken breast strips quickly sautéed, and then flavored with an easy pan sauce made with lemon juice, parsley, and capers. Serve it over pasta to enjoy the sauce, alongside a tossed salad.

1¼ pounds boneless, skinless chicken breast halves
⅓ cup all-purpose flour
Salt and freshly ground black pepper to taste
½ cup Augmented Oil (page 15)
3 tablespoons Bong Butter (page 14)
1 cup chicken stock
⅓ cup freshly squeezed lemon juice
¼ cup chopped fresh parsley
½ teaspoon dried oregano
3 tablespoons capers, drained and rinsed

YIELD: 4 to 6 servings
ACTIVE TIME: 10 minutes
START TO FINISH: 25 minutes

1. Rinse chicken and pat dry with paper towels. Trim chicken of all visible fat. Place chicken between two sheets of plastic wrap, and pound to an even thickness of ½ inch. Cut breasts into 2-inch strips. Season flour to taste with salt and pepper. Dust chicken with seasoned flour, shaking off any excess.

2. Heat oil and butter in a large skillet over medium-high heat. Add chicken and brown on both sides, turning pieces with tongs. Remove chicken from the pan, and set aside.

3. Add stock, lemon juice, parsley, oregano, and capers to the skillet. Bring to a boil, reduce the heat to medium-high, and reduce sauce for 5 minutes. Return chicken to the skillet, and cook for an additional 5 minutes, or until chicken is cooked through and no longer pink. Season to taste with salt and pepper. Serve immediately.

NOTE: The dish can be prepared up to 2 days in advance and refrigerated, tightly covered. Reheat it, covered, over low heat until hot.

VARIATIONS:
- Substitute thick white-fleshed fish fillets for the chicken, and seafood stock for the chicken stock.
- Substitute veal scallops for the chicken.

Capers are the flower bud of a low bush native to the Mediterranean. After harvest they're sun-dried and pickled in vinegar. The best capers are the tiny ones from France, and while they are customarily packed in brine they can also be bought packed in coarse salt. However you buy them, rinse them well before using them.

Rasta Weed Chicken Wraps

The smoky flavor of chipotle chiles, which are smoked jalapeño chiles, is balanced by the fresh aroma of cilantro for a sauce seasoned with shake that moistens this wrap sandwich filled with chicken as well as red onion.

½ cup Amazing Mayo (page 16)
¼ cup chopped fresh cilantro
1 or 2 chipotle chiles in adobo sauce, finely chopped
4 (10-inch) flour or whole-wheat tortillas
8 leaves romaine lettuce, rinsed and dried
½ small red onion, peeled and thinly sliced
¾ pound thinly sliced cooked chicken

YIELD: 4 servings
ACTIVE TIME: 15 minutes
START TO FINISH: 15 minutes

1. Combine mayo, cilantro, and chiles in a small mixing bowl, and stir well. Set aside.

2. Soften tortillas, if necessary, by wrapping them in plastic wrap and heating them in a microwave oven on High (100 percent power) for 10 to 15 seconds, or until pliable.

3. Arrange lettuce leaves on tortillas, and spread dressing on top of lettuce. Layer red onion and chicken on bottom half of each tortilla. Tuck sides of tortillas over filling, and roll gently but firmly beginning at the filled side. Cut in half on the diagonal prior to serving.

NOTE: The dressing can be made up to 1 day in advance and refrigerated, tightly covered.

Deviled Diablo Chicken

Back in the nineteenth century something that was "deviled" meant it had some assertive flavor, usually mustard. That's why both this mustard-coated chicken and eggs flavored with mustard was called "deviled." It's the coating on this chicken that gives you a good dose of dope, and it's great cold, too.

1 (3½ to 4-pound) frying chicken, cut into serving pieces, with each breast half cut in half crosswise

10 tablespoons Bong Butter (page 14), melted

Salt and freshly ground black pepper to taste

⅓ cup Dijon mustard

3 scallions, white parts and 3 inches of green tops, finely chopped

¾ teaspoon dried thyme

3 cups plain breadcrumbs

YIELD: **4 to 6 servings**

ACTIVE TIME: **20 minutes**

START TO FINISH: **1 ¼ hours**

NOTE: The chicken can be prepared up to 2 days in advance and refrigerated, tightly covered.

1. Preheat the oven to 400ºF, and line a 10 x 14-inch baking pan with heavy-duty aluminum foil.

2. Rinse chicken and pat dry with paper towels. Brush chicken with butter, and sprinkle with salt and pepper. Bake chicken, skin side down, for 15 minutes.

3. While chicken bakes, combine mustard, scallions, thyme, and 3 tablespoons of remaining butter in a mixing bowl, and whisk well. Place breadcrumbs in a shallow bowl or on a sheet of plastic wrap or waxed paper.

4. Remove chicken pieces from the oven, and allow them to cool for 5 minutes. Using tongs, roll chicken in mustard mixture, and then place into crumbs, patting pieces so that crumbs adhere. Return chicken to the baking pan, skin side up.

5. Return chicken to the oven, and bake for 25 to 35 minutes, or until chicken registers 165ºF on an instant-read thermometer and is cooked through and no longer pink. Serve hot, at room temperature, or chilled.

YIELD: 4 to 6 servings
ACTIVE TIME: 15 minutes
START TO FINISH: 25 minutes

Power of Pepper Pasta Carbonara

It takes longer for the water to come to a boil to cook the pasta than it does to create this classic Italian dish that's spicy with black pepper and rich from eggs and cheese. A tossed salad is all you need to complete the meal.

⅔ pound spaghetti
¾ pound bacon, sliced into ½-inch strips
⅔ cup Augmented Oil (page 15)
6 garlic cloves, minced
Freshly ground black pepper to taste (at least 1½ teaspoons)
6 large eggs, well beaten
1½ cups freshly grated Parmesan cheese
Salt to taste

64

1. Bring a large pot of salted water to a boil. Add pasta, and cook according to package directions until al dente. Drain, and set aside.

2. While water heats, place bacon in a large heavy skillet over medium-high heat. Cook, stirring occasionally, for 5 to 7 minutes, or until crisp. Remove bacon from the skillet with a slotted spoon, and set aside. Discard bacon grease from the pan. Add oil, garlic, and pepper, and cook for 30 seconds. Return bacon to the pan, and turn off heat.

3. Add drained pasta to the skillet, and cook over medium heat for 1 minute. Remove the pan from the stove, and stir in eggs. Cover the pan for 2 minutes to allow eggs to thicken, but do not put the pan back on the stove or they will scramble. Add cheese, and season to taste with salt and additional pepper. Serve immediately.

The last place you want your money going is to an expensive visit from the plumber, and bacon grease is notorious for clogging kitchen plumbing, even if it's put down the sink with the hot water running. Rinse out empty tin cans, and keep them under the sink. Pour unwanted bacon fat into a bowl, and after it cools dispose of it in the container.

Bamba Baked Macaroni and Cheese with Ham

Macaroni and cheese is beloved by every generation—past and present, and I'm sure future, too. The paprika and mustard add a bit of kick to this version, and you'll get a kick from the sauce, too.

⅔ pound elbow macaroni
6 tablespoons Bong Butter (page 14)
3 tablespoons all-purpose flour
1 tablespoon paprika
¼ teaspoon cayenne, or to taste
⅔ cup chicken stock
1½ cups Bhang Booster (page 17)
1 pound grated sharp cheddar cheese, divided
1 tablespoon Dijon mustard
¾ pound baked ham, trimmed of fat and cut into ½-inch dice
Salt and freshly ground black pepper to taste

YIELD: **4 to 6 servings**
ACTIVE TIME: **15 minutes**
START TO FINISH: **35 minutes**

1. Preheat the oven to 400°F, and grease a 10 x 14-inch baking pan. Bring a large pot of salted water to a boil. Add macaroni, and cook according to package directions until al dente. Drain, and place in the prepared pan.

2. While pasta cooks, heat butter in saucepan over low heat. Stir in flour, paprika, and cayenne, and cook, stirring constantly, for 2 minutes. Whisk in stock, and bring to a boil over medium-high heat, whisking constantly. Reduce the heat to low, and simmer 2 minutes. Stir in Bhang Booster and all but ½ cup of grated cheese, and stir until cheese melts. Stir in mustard and ham, and season to taste with salt and pepper. Pour sauce over macaroni, and stir well.

3. Cover the pan with foil, and bake for 10 minutes. Uncover the pan, sprinkle with remaining cheese, and bake for an additional 10 to 15 minutes, or until bubbly. Serve immediately.

NOTE: The dish can be prepared up to 2 days in advance and refrigerated, tightly covered. Reheat it, covered, in a 350°F oven for 20 to 25 minutes, or until hot.

VARIATIONS:
- Omit the ham and substitute vegetable stock for the chicken stock for a vegetarian dish.
- Substitute roast turkey or chicken for the ham.
- Substitute jalapeño Jack for the cheddar cheese for a spicier dish.

While the American song "Yankee Doole Dandy" has the famous line about "stuck a feather in his cap and called it macaroni," the macaroni in question was not pasta! In the mid-eighteenth century the so-called "Macaroni Wig" was the height of foppish fashion in London. The meaning of the lyric is that the unsophisticated Yankee thought that a feather was the same look.

Hooch Ham and Swag Sweet Potato Salad

Ham and sweet potatoes hold a place of honor on many Southern dinner tables, and their flavor blends beautifully in this salad, too. Chopped pickles and Dijon mustard add flavor accents to the dish. And don't skimp on the dressing; that's where the hooch is hidden.

1½ pounds sweet potatoes, scrubbed
¼ cup cider vinegar
2 tablespoons Dijon mustard
Salt and freshly ground black pepper to taste
2 garlic cloves, minced
⅔ cup Augmented Oil (page 15)
2 cups diced baked ham
¼ small red onion, finely chopped
1 small green bell pepper, seeds and ribs removed, and finely chopped
¼ cup finely chopped sweet pickles
4 to 6 cups bite-sized pieces mixed salad greens, rinsed and dried

YIELD: **4 to 6** servings
ACTIVE TIME: **20** minutes
START TO FINISH: **35** minutes, including **15** minutes for cooling

1. Bring a pot of salted water to a boil over high heat. Quarter sweet potatoes lengthwise, and cut quarters into 1-inch sections. Place sweet potatoes in the saucepan, and boil for 10 minutes, or until potatoes are tender. Drain and run under cold water. Peel potatoes when cool enough to handle. Cut potatoes into cubes, and place in a mixing bowl.

2. Combine vinegar, mustard, salt, pepper, and garlic in a jar with a tight-fitting lid, and shake well. Add oil, and shake well again. Add dressing to potatoes along with ham, onion, green pepper, and pickles. Toss gently, and season to taste with salt and pepper.

3. To serve, arrange greens on individual plates or on a large platter and top with salad. Salad can be served at room temperature or chilled.

NOTE: The salad can be made 1 day in advance and refrigerated, tightly covered with plastic wrap.

chapter 4

SWEETS FROM THE STOVE

I wanted to make *Stoner Snacks* a book that everyone could enjoy, not just people who live in a place with a room called a kitchen. Maybe your living situation is such that cooking is a combo of what can be nuked in the microwave and what can come off of your hotplate. If that's the case, then this is the chapter for you.

None of these recipes have a degree sign anywhere to be found. Some of them require refrigeration, but if that's a problem, too, just make them when it's winter and you can put them out on the fire escape.

You'll find some seriously sweet treats here, ranging from variations on fudge to no-bake cookie kinds of dishes to sauces to top anything and everything from hot cakes to ice cream. All these recipes start with Bong Butter (page 14), the mainstay of the cannabis kitchen, and many get their creaminess from a good shot of Bhang Booster (page 17), too.

Penuche

Pronounced puh-KNOW-chee, this Mexican butterscotch fudge is the epitome of what you're craving as a sweet munchies. And its combo of "leaded" ingredients keeps the high movin' right along.

YIELD: 6 to 8 servings
ACTIVE TIME: 30 minutes
START TO FINISH: 1 hour, including 30 minutes for chilling

⅔ cup Bhang Booster (page 17)
2 cups firmly packed light brown sugar
12 tablespoons Bong Butter (page 14)
Pinch of salt
1 teaspoon pure vanilla extract, preferably Mexican
1½ cups confectioners' sugar

1. Combine Bhang Booster, brown sugar, butter, salt, and vanilla in a saucepan, and bring to a boil over medium heat, stirring to dissolve sugar.

2. Reduce the heat to medium-low, and simmer mixture for 15 to 20 minutes, or until it looks thicker and syrupy.

3. Remove the pan from the heat, and beat in the confectioners' sugar with an electric mixer at low speed. Beat for 3 to 5 minutes, or until mixture is thick and smooth. Scrape penuche into a 9 x 9-inch pan, and refrigerate for 30 minutes, or until firm. Cut into squares.

NOTE: The fudge can be prepared up to 1 week in advance and refrigerated, tightly covered once chilled.

The only difference between butterscotch and caramel is that butterscotch starts with brown sugar rather than white sugar. Most Mexican and Latin American recipes use light brown sugar because it's the closest to the region's unrefined sugar.

SUGAR

Kona Gold Coconut Chocolate Fudge

Chocolate and coconut is one of my favorite combinations, and if you like it in a candy bar you'll love it in this fudge. It's creamy and intensely flavored. You'll go bonkers for it even before you go bonkers.

6 (2-ounce) chocolate-covered coconut candy bars
2 cups granulated sugar
12 tablespoons Bong Butter (page 14)
¾ cup Bhang Booster (page 17)
2 cups semisweet chocolate chips
1 (7-ounce) jar marshmallow cream
1 teaspoon coconut extract

YIELD: 10 to 12 servings
ACTIVE TIME: 10 minutes
START TO FINISH: 1¼ hours

1. Line a 9 x 9-inch pan with aluminum foil, allowing it to extend at least 3 inches over the sides. Cut candy bars into ½-inch slices, and set aside.

2. Combine sugar, butter, and Bhang Booster in a saucepan. Bring to a boil over medium heat, stirring occasionally. Cook, stirring frequently, for 3 to 4 minutes, or until mixture reaches 234ºF (soft ball stage) on a candy thermometer.

3. Remove the pan from the heat, and stir in chocolate chips, marshmallow cream, and coconut extract.

4. Pour half of mixture into the pan, and top with half of candy slices. Repeat with remaining chocolate and candy slices.

5. Chill for 1 hour, or until set. Lift fudge out of the pan using the foil, and cut into squares.

NOTE: The fudge can be refrigerated for up to 1 week, tightly covered.

VARIATION:
- Substitute almond extract for the coconut extract, and add 3/4 cup chopped almonds to the fudge mixture.

YIELD: 6 to 8 servings
ACTIVE TIME: 20 minutes
START TO FINISH: 4½ hours

Boozy Cheeba Chocolate Loaf

This chilled dessert is sort of like the richest chocolate mousse you can imagine, with lots of crunchy cookies adding a whole wonderful textural thing. It's so good and rich that you'll be tempted to eat it right away, but it's even better once chilled.

8 ounces high-quality bittersweet chocolate, chopped

¼ cup Amaretto or other almond-flavored liqueur, treated according to the formulation for Booze with Buzz (page 18)

10 tablespoons Bong Butter (page 14), softened

⅔ cup confectioners' sugar

½ teaspoon pure almond extract

Pinch of salt

1 cup heavy whipping cream

1 (8-ounce) package almond-flavored butter cookies, broken into ½-inch pieces

1. Line a 9 x 5-inch loaf pan with plastic wrap, allowing it to extend at least 3 inches over the sides.

2. Combine chocolate and liqueur in a small microwave-safe dish. Microwave at Medium (50 percent power) for 1 minute. Stir, and repeat at 15 second intervals until chocolate melts and mixture is smooth. Set aside to cool for 10 minutes.

3. While chocolate cools, combine butter and sugar in a mixing bowl. Beat at low speed with an electric mixer until combined. Increase the speed to high, and beat until light and fluffy. Beat in almond extract and salt. Fold in cooled chocolate mixture.

4. Place cream in a well-chilled mixing bowl, and beat at high speed with an electric mixer until stiff peaks form.

5. Fold cream and broken cookies into chocolate mixture. Scrape mixture into the loaf pan, evening the top with a spatula. Chill loaf, covered, for at least 4 hours.

6. To serve, invert the loaf pan onto a platter, and discard plastic wrap. Cut into slices, and serve chilled.

NOTE: The loaf can be refrigerated for up to 4 days or frozen for up to 2 months.

VARIATIONS:
- Substitute rum for the Amaretto and ginger snap cookies for the almond butter cookies.
- Substitute white chocolate for the bittersweet chocolate, Gran Marnier for the Amaretto, plain butter cookies for the almond cookies, and add 1 tablespoon grated orange zest to chocolate mixture.

Chilling out is more than a way to lead your life. It's also the way to get the best whipped cream. If you use chilled beaters on your electric mixer or your whisk, and you chill the bowl, the cream will form nice stiff peaks in about half the time it takes with the equipment at room temperature. This is even more important in the summer, when room temperature can be really high.

YIELD: 6 to 8 servings
ACTIVE TIME: 20 minutes
START TO FINISH: 1½ hours

Head-Frying Fried Cookies

These crispy cookies are like tiny doughnuts, only with a richer flavor. Once dusted with confectioners' sugar, they're like miniature snowflakes playing on your tongue.

3 large eggs
¼ cup whole milk
¾ cup granulated sugar
8 tablespoons Bong Butter (page 14), melted
1 teaspoon baking soda
1 teaspoon pure vanilla extract
½ teaspoon salt
½ teaspoon freshly ground nutmeg
3½ cups all-purpose flour, plus additional for rolling
Vegetable oil for frying
1 cup confectioners' sugar for dusting

1. Combine eggs, milk, sugar, and butter in a mixing bowl, and whisk well. Whisk in baking soda, vanilla, salt, and nutmeg. Add flour, and mix well until it forms a soft dough. Refrigerate dough, tightly covered, for at least 1 hour, or up to 3 days.

2. Dust a counter and rolling pin with flour. Roll out dough to an even thickness of ¼ inch. Cut dough into strips 1 inch wide. Cut strips on a diagonal at 3-inch intervals to form diamond shapes.

3. Pour oil to a depth of 1½ inches in a deep-sided saucepan. Heat oil to a temperature of 375ºF on a candy/deep fry thermometer. Add a few cookies at a time to the pan, turning cookies with a slotted spoon to brown on both sides.

4. Drain cookies on paper towels, and sift confectioners' sugar on them. Serve immediately.

NOTE: The cookies can be fried up to 2 days in advance and kept in an airtight container at room temperature. Do not dust with sugar if storing. Reheat the cookies in a 250ºF oven for 3 to 5 minutes, then dust with sugar and serve.

Don't have a rolling pin? Or your rolling pin is keeping your window propped open? No problem. Cover a glass wine bottle or any sort of round bottle with aluminum foil. Voilà! You've got a rolling pin!

Crazy Weed "Cracker Jack"

The prize from this sweet and crunchy treat is the high you're going to feel after eating a few sweet and buttery bites. This recipe is enough reason to own a microwave.

⅔ cup popcorn kernels (the equivalent of 1 large bag microwave popcorn)

2 cups whole roasted nuts, some combination of almonds, walnuts, pecans, cashews, peanuts

1½ cups firmly packed light brown sugar

¾ cup light corn syrup

12 tablespoons Bong Butter (page 14)

1 teaspoon pure vanilla extract

¾ teaspoon baking soda

YIELD: 8 to 10 servings

ACTIVE TIME: 15 minutes

START TO FINISH: 25 minutes

1. Cook popcorn. If using microwave popcorn cook according to instructions, and if using loose kernels, pop with oil in a skillet. Pour it into a large mixing bowl, and shake it well so

that the unpopped kernels sink to the bottom of the bowl. Then transfer the popcorn to another bowl, discarding the unpopped kernels. Add nuts to the bowl with the popcorn.

2. Combine brown sugar, corn syrup, and butter in a saucepan. Bring to a boil over medium heat, stirring to dissolve the sugar. Reduce the heat to low, and cook for 4 minutes without stirring. Stir vanilla and baking soda into mixture.

3. Slowly pour the syrup over popcorn and nuts, and stir to coat everything well.

4. Place mixture in a brown paper bag, and place in the microwave. Microwave on High (100 percent power) for 1 1/2 minutes. Turn the bag over, and microwave for an additional 1 minute. Remove the bag from the oven, and cut it open. Allow mixture to cool for 5 minutes.

NOTE: The popcorn will keep at room temperature in an airtight container for up to 10 days. If you want to bake it rather than nuke it, bake it at 250°F for 45 minutes in a greased roasting pan, stirring it every 15 minutes.

While the prototype for Cracker Jacks was introduced at the World's Fair in Chicago in 1893, the caramel-coated popcorn with nuts became immortalized in 1908 with the song "Take Me Out to the Ball Game," the third line of which is "Buy me some peanuts and Cracker Jack." Inducing sales with the prize in every box followed four years later.

Crispy Critter Peanut Butter Cereal Bars

These are an adult and augmented version of those treats that everyone under the age of fifty ate as a kid. You've got your cereal, you've got your marshmallow, and in this case you've also got rich peanut butter, crispy peanuts, and a touch of cinnamon.

8 tablespoons Bong Butter (page 14)
1 (7-ounce) jar marshmallow cream
¾ cup crunchy peanut butter
½ teaspoon ground cinnamon
½ cup chopped roasted peanuts
3 cups puffed rice cereal
3 cups corn flakes
Vegetable oil spray

YIELD: 4 to 6 servings
ACTIVE TIME: 15 minutes
START TO FINISH: 25 minutes

NOTE: While these are best when eaten on the day they are made, they can be stored up to 2 days in an airtight container at room temperature.

Variations:
• Use all puffed rice cereal or all cornflakes instead of a mixture of the two.
• Add 1 cup miniature chocolate chips to mixture or spread melted chocolate over the top.

1. Grease a 9 x 13-inch pan with vegetable oil spray.

2. Combine butter, marshmallow cream, peanut butter, and cinnamon in a saucepan. Cook, stirring frequently, until mixture is smooth and hot.

3. Combine peanuts, rice cereal, and corn flakes in a large mixing bowl, and pour hot mixture over cereal. Stir until well coated, and press mixture into the prepared pan. Cool for 10 to 15 minutes, or until room temperature. Cut into pieces, and serve immediately.

Caramel Rum Funky Fondue

This is one of my favorite fondues because I adore the rich and buttery taste of caramel sauce. It seems to complement just about every fruit.

2 cups granulated sugar

½ cup water

10 tablespoons Bong Butter (page 14), softened and cut into small pieces

2 cups heavy cream

¼ cup rum, treated according to the formulation for Booze with Buzz (page 18)

1 teaspoon pure vanilla extract

For serving: Banana chunks, apple slices, dried apricots, donut holes, squares of waffle, cubes of angel food cake, cubes of pound cake, cubes of brownie, coconut macaroons, or sugar cookies.

YIELD: 4 to 6 servings

ACTIVE TIME: 15 minutes

START TO FINISH: 30 minutes

1. Combine sugar and water in a 1-quart saucepan. Bring to a simmer over medium heat, swirling occasionally. Cover the pan, raise the high to medium-high, and cook until the liquid gives off thick large bubbles. Remove the cover and cook until the syrup reaches a golden brown.

2. Remove the pan from the heat, and stir in butter with a long-handled wooden spoon. Add cream, stirring constantly, and then add rum and vanilla. Return the pan to a low flame, and stir constantly until the lumps have melted and the syrup is smooth.

3. To serve, transfer fondue to a fondue pot or other pot with a heat source.

NOTE: The fondue can be prepared up to 4 hours in advance and kept at room temperature. Reheat it over very low heat, stirring frequently, or in a microwave oven.

VARIATION:

• Substitute a fruit- or nut-flavored liqueur for the rum.

Maple Raisin Reefer Rice Pudding

Rice pudding is a great winter dessert. It's thick and rich; it's comforting and not edgy. And you'll be on one good high with this version of this homey dish. It's laced with loco weed.

2 cups Bhang Booster (page 17)
2 cups whole milk
1 cup Arborio rice
½ cup pure maple syrup
8 tablespoons Bong Butter (page 14), divided
½ teaspoon salt
¾ cup raisins
2 large egg yolks
1 cup heavy whipping cream
Apple pie spice (optional)

YIELD: 8 to 10 servings
ACTIVE TIME: 15 minutes
START TO FINISH: 50 minutes

1. Combine Bhang Booster, milk, rice, maple syrup, 4 tablespoons butter, and salt in a saucepan, and bring to a boil over medium heat, stirring occasionally. Reduce the heat to low, and simmer rice, covered, for 20 to 30 minutes, or until rice is tender. Stir mixture occasionally, especially toward the end of the simmering time, to prevent it from sticking on the bottom of the pot. Stir in remaining butter and raisins, and remove the pan from the heat.

NOTE: The rice pudding can be prepared up to 4 days in advance and refrigerated, tightly covered.

2. While rice cooks, whisk egg yolks and cream together. Add cream mixture to the saucepan, and stir well. Cover the pan, and allow pudding to sit for 10 minutes.

3. Serve hot, at room temperature, or chilled. Sprinkle each serving with apple pie spice, if using.

Arborio is a short-grained Italian rice with high starch content, which is why it's really good for making risotto. If you don't have any around, it's best to use an Asian sushi rice or a domestic short-grain rice for rice puddings. If you use a long-grain, converted rice, it won't get creamy enough.

Steamy Orange Christmas Bud Pudding

Are your holiday dinners with family boring? Start with a big slice of this dessert, derived from English traditions, and you'll forget all about that dry turkey or your obnoxious uncle. And it's full of healthy dried fruits, too.

½ cup Grand Marnier or other orange-flavored liqueur, treated according to the formulation for Booze with Buzz (page 18)

1 cup raisins

½ cup dried currants

½ cup chopped candied fruit or additional dried fruits

12 tablespoons Bong Butter (page 14), melted

¾ cup orange marmalade

¼ cup firmly packed light brown sugar

2 large eggs, lightly beaten

1 teaspoon baking soda

½ teaspoon salt

1 ¼ cups all-purpose flour, divided

Hashish Hard Sauce (opposite page)

YIELD: 6 to 8 servings
ACTIVE TIME: 20 minutes
START TO FINISH: 2½ hours

1. Grease a steep-sided mixing bowl, and bring 5 inches of water to a boil in a stockpot large enough to hold the mixing bowl.

2. Place Grand Marnier in a mixing bowl, and add raisins, currants, and dried fruit. Toss to coat fruit evenly, and allow to sit for 10 minutes.

3. Combine butter, marmalade, sugar, eggs, baking soda, and salt in a large mixing bowl. Whisk well. Drain fruit, adding any remaining liqueur to batter.

4. Stir 1 cup flour into batter, and stir well. Toss drained fruit with remaining flour, and fold into batter. Scrape batter into the mixing bowl, smoothing the top with a spatula. Cover the bowl with a double layer of heavy-duty aluminum foil, crimping it around the edge of the bowl.

5. Place a heatproof trivet in the bottom of the stockpot, and place pudding on top of the trivet. Cover the pot, and steam the pudding over low heat for 2 hours. Check the level of the water occasionally and add more as necessary.

NOTE: The pudding can be prepared up to 5 days in advance and kept at room temperature. Reheat it, encased in foil, in a 300°F oven for 25 to 30 minutes, or until hot.

6. Remove pudding from the pan, and allow it to sit for 5 minutes. Discard the foil, and invert pudding onto a platter. Serve hot, accompanied by Hashish Hard Sauce.

By tossing the dried fruit with a bit of the flour they don't all sink to the bottom while the pudding is steaming. The flour forms glue with the batter around it.

Hashish Hard Sauce

Rich and buttery, this sauce has the consistency of a spread. This souped-up sauce makes any warm dessert—from a cake or pie to Steamy Orange Christmas Bud Pudding (opposite page)—a mind-expanding treat.

8 tablespoons Bong Butter (page 14), softened
1½ cups confectioners' sugar
¼ teaspoon pure vanilla extract
2 to 3 tablespoons brandy, rum, or bourbon, treated according to the formulation for Booze with Buzz (page 18)

YIELD: 6 servings
ACTIVE TIME: 5 minutes
START TO FINISH: 5 minutes

NOTE: Make up to 1 week in advance and refrigerate, tightly covered. Allow it to sit at room temperature for 30 minutes before serving, or microwave it on Medium (50 percent power) for 30 seconds, or until softened.

1. Combine the butter, confectioners' sugar, vanilla, and brandy in a mixing bowl. Beat at low speed with an electric mixer to combine. Increase the speed to high, and beat for 2 minutes until light and fluffy.

2. Serve at room temperature on top of warm desserts.

Crazy Caramel Sauce

Caramel is sugar and water cooked together to a high
temperature until syrupy. Once that's done, just add some
butter and cream and you've got caramel sauce. It's great on
ice cream, or just out of the jar once it chills.

3 cups granulated sugar
1 cup water
8 tablespoons Bong Butter (page 14),
   cut into small pieces
1 cup heavy cream
1 cup Bhang Booster (page 17)
2 teaspoons pure vanilla extract

YIELD: 6 to 8 servings
ACTIVE TIME: 15 minutes
START TO FINISH: 15 minutes

1. Combine sugar and water in a 2-quart saucepan, and bring to a boil over medium-high heat. Swirl the pan by the handle but do not stir. Raise the heat to high, and allow syrup to cook until it reaches a walnut brown color, swirling the pot by the handle frequently.

2. Remove the pan from the heat, and stir in butter, cream, and Bhang Booster with a long-handled spoon; the mixture will bubble furiously at first. Return the pan to low heat and stir until lumps melt and sauce is smooth. Stir in vanilla, and transfer to a jar. Serve hot, room temperature, or cold.

NOTE: The sauce can be refrigerated up to 1 week, tightly covered.

VARIATION:
• Decrease the vanilla to ½ teaspoon and add 2 tablespoons brandy, rum, or a liqueur.

To clean a pan that has been used to make caramel sauce is to fill the pan with water and place it back on the stove. Stir as the water comes to a boil and all the caramel bits will melt.

Aunt Mary Jane's Lemon Curd

Luscious ripe summer fruits can get you high just by looking at them, and this sauce is a perfect topping to bring some loco into your life. If you want to make it look fancy, spread it out in a baked piecrust, and top it with some fruit.

YIELD: **4 to 6 servings**
ACTIVE TIME: **15 minutes**
START TO FINISH: **1 hour, including 45 minutes for chilling**

4 large eggs
1½ cups granulated sugar
1 cup freshly squeezed lemon juice
2 tablespoons grated lemon zest
Pinch of salt
12 tablespoons Bong Butter (page 14), cut into small pieces

1. Combine eggs and sugar in a saucepan, and beat with a whisk until the color lightens and the mixture thickens. Add lemon juice, lemon zest, and salt; beat well. Add the butter, and whisk again.

2. Place the pan over medium heat, and cook, whisking constantly, until butter melts and mixture thickens, about 10 minutes. Remove the pan from the heat, and scrape the curd into a mixing bowl. Press a sheet of plastic wrap directly into the surface to prevent a skin from forming.

3. Refrigerate the curd for 45 minutes, or until chilled.

NOTE: The curd can be prepared up to 5 days in advance and refrigerated, tightly covered.

VARIATION:
- Substitute lime juice and lime zest for the lemon juice and lemon zest

Always grate the zest off of citrus fruits before you squeeze the juice out of them; a whole fruit is easier handle because it's firmer. To get the most juice out of your citrus, roll them hard on a counter before you squeeze them. The pressure helps to break down the fibers.

Hooched Up Hot Banana Splits with Chocolate Sauce

The sweetness of bananas is accentuated when they're cooked, and their texture turns soft and velvety. For these sundaes, the bananas are cooked in a chocolate and caramel sauce spiked with two forms of cannabis treats.

6 tablespoons Bong Butter (page 14)
4 ripe bananas, sliced diagonally into ½-inch-thick slices
½ cup firmly packed dark brown sugar
¾ cup Bhang Booster (page 17)
4 ounces bittersweet chocolate, finely chopped
¼ teaspoon pure vanilla extract
1 pint vanilla ice cream, softened

YIELD: 4 to 6 servings
ACTIVE TIME: 15 minutes
START TO FINISH: 15 minutes

1. Melt butter in a large skillet over medium-high heat. Add bananas, and sprinkle sugar over bananas. Cook bananas, turning gently with a slotted spatula, for 3 minutes. Remove bananas from the skillet with a slotted spatula, and keep warm.

NOTE: The bananas can be cooked and the sauce can be completed up to 6 hours in advance. Reheat the bananas in the sauce before serving.

2. Add Bhang Booster, chocolate, and vanilla to the skillet. Cook over medium heat, stirring constantly, for 2 minutes, or until caramel dissolves.

3. To serve, place ice cream in dessert bowls and top with banana slices and sauce.

If you have bananas that are too ripe to eat and are perfect for a cake, you don't have to bake them right at that second. Freeze the bananas right in the skins, then defrost and mash them at a later time.

SUGAR

chapter 5

YUMMIES FROM THE OVEN

The lore about Alice B. Toklas' famous brownies is responsible for launching the category of stoner snacks, and no book devoted to them would be complete without a chapter on ballistic baked goods with some bamba. Buttery richness is what unites the sweet treats that will be coming out of your oven. And buttery richness in this case is due to lots of Bong Butter (page 14), that wonderful stuff that coats your tummy with THC.

While there are a few cookies leading off the chapter, a good portion of the recipes is for cakes. The reason is that these cakes take only minutes to prepare, and then you've got a lot of food with fu around.

Cookie Dough Cache

Cookie doughs are not only easy to make, they're just about indestructible. You can successfully freeze cookie dough and bake off individual cookies or a whole batch at a moment's notice, like when your friends are walking in the door and you decide that a cannabis creation is in order.

If you want to freeze a whole batch of dough, do so in a heavy resealable plastic bag. Allow it to thaw overnight in the refrigerator. But I find it's much easier to freeze individual dough balls.

Cover a baking sheet with plastic wrap, and form the proper size balls of dough on the cookie sheet. You can place them very close together because they're not going to spread. Once they are frozen solid, transfer them to a heavy resealable plastic bag. It's not necessary to allow time for frozen dough balls to thaw. Just add 2 to 3 minutes to the baking time of the cookie.

Ode to Alice B. Toklas Marble Fudge Brownies

No book titled *Stoner Snacks* should be published without a recipe for a boosted brownie! I adore the combination of chocolate and cream cheese, and these brownies deliver both.

8 tablespoons Bong Butter (page 14)
4 ounces semisweet chocolate, chopped
3 large eggs, at room temperature, divided
1 cup granulated sugar, divided
½ cup all-purpose flour
Pinch of salt
1 (8-ounce) package cream cheese, softened
½ teaspoon pure vanilla extract

YIELD: 12 brownies
ACTIVE TIME: 15 minutes
START TO FINISH: 1 hour

1. Preheat the oven to 350°F. Grease and flour a 9 x 9-inch square cake pan.

2. Melt butter and chocolate over low heat or in a microwave oven. Stir to combine, and set aside for 5 minutes to cool.

3. Combine 2 eggs and ¾ cup sugar in mixing bowl. Beat with an electric mixer on medium speed for 1 minute, or until well combined. Add cooled chocolate mixture, and beat for 1 minute. Add flour and salt and beat at low speed until just blended.

4. In another bowl, combine cream cheese, remaining ¼ cup sugar, remaining 1 egg, and vanilla. Beat with an electric mixer on medium speed for 2 minutes, or until light and fluffy. Spread chocolate batter into the prepared pan. Top with cream cheese batter and swirl layers together with a fork.

5. Bake for 35 minutes, or until the top is springy to the touch. Cool brownies on a wire cooling rack, then cut into 12 pieces.

NOTE: The brownies can be made up to 3 days in advance and kept at room temperature, tightly covered with plastic wrap. They also freeze well for up to 1 month, so make a double batch.

Alice Babette Toklas, a native of San Francisco, met Gertrude Stein the first day she arrived in Paris in 1907. She was Stein's confidante and lover, as well as partner in her famous soirees, until Stein's death in 1946. Stein published her own memoirs with the title *The Autobiography of Alice B. Toklas* in 1933, but the recipe for hash-laced brownies was part of Alice's own book, *The Alice B. Toklas Cookbook*, which was published in 1954.

Cheeba Chocolate Coconut Bars

I really grove out on those candy bars that are chocolate-covered coconut, so I decided to turn them into a cookie bar with that special ingredient that makes them ever so much tastier for a few hours.

1 cup (16 tablespoons) Bong Butter (page 14)
¾ cup granulated sugar
¾ cup firmly packed light brown sugar
2 large eggs
1 teaspoon pure almond extract
¼ cup unsweetened cocoa powder
1 teaspoon baking soda
½ teaspoon salt
2 cups all-purpose flour
1 cup miniature chocolate chips
1 (14-ounce) can sweetened condensed milk
1 cup firmly packed unsweetened coconut flakes

YIELD: 8 to 10 servings
ACTIVE TIME: 10 minutes
START TO FINISH: 35 minutes

1. Preheat the oven to 375ºF, and grease a 9 x 13-inch baking pan.

2. Combine butter, sugar, and brown sugar in a mixing bowl, and beat at medium speed with an electric mixer until light and fluffy. Beat in eggs, and almond extract, and beat well again.

3. Beat in cocoa powder, baking soda, and salt at medium speed. Reduce the speed to low, and add flour. Fold in chocolate chips.

4. Spread batter into the prepared pan. Combine condensed milk and coconut in a small bowl, and stir well. Spread as an even layer on top of chocolate dough.

5. Bake for 25 to 30 minutes, or until a toothpick inserted comes out clean. Cool the pan on a cooling rack, and then cut into bars.

NOTE: The bars can be prepared up to 4 days in advance and kept in an airtight container at room temperature.

The Aztecs first discovered chocolate, and our word comes from the Aztec xocolatl, which means "bitter water." Famed King Montezuma believed chocolate was an aphrodisiac and is reported to have consumed some 50 cups a day.

Think tropics and then think coconut. The name first appeared in English in the mid-sixteenth century. It comes from the Spanish and Portuguese word coco, which means "monkey face." The earlier explorers thought the three round markings at the base of the coconut looked like eyes and a mouth. In addition to being a food, also prized for its water, coconuts were the currency of the Nicobar Islands of the Indian Ocean until the early part of the twentieth century.

Butterscotch Blondies

While blondies are the name given to brownie-like cookies made without chocolate, these blondies are laced with blonde, so you'll really get off on their heady flavor.

12 tablespoons Bong Butter (page 14)
1½ cups firmly packed light brown sugar
2 large eggs
½ teaspoon pure vanilla extract
1½ teaspoons baking powder
½ teaspoon salt
2⅓ cups all-purpose flour
⅔ cup butterscotch chips

YIELD: 6 to 8 servings
ACTIVE TIME: 15 minutes
START TO FINISH: 50 minutes

1. Preheat the oven to 350ºF, and grease a 9 x 13-inch baking pan.

2. Combine butter and sugar in a small saucepan. Place over medium heat and cook, stirring frequently, until butter melts and mixture is smooth. Scrape mixture into a mixing bowl. Cool to room temperature.

3. Whisk eggs and vanilla into mixture, beating until smooth. Beat in baking powder and salt, and then flour. Fold in butterscotch chips.

NOTE: The bars can be prepared up to 4 days in advance and kept in an airtight container at room temperature.

4. Scrape batter into the pan, and bake for 20 minutes, or until a toothpick inserted in the center comes out clean. Cool the pan on a cooling rack, and then cut into bars.

Brown sugar is granulated sugar mixed with molasses, and the darker the color, the more pronounced the molasses flavor. If a recipe calls for dark brown sugar, and you only have light brown sugar, add 2 tablespoons molasses per ½ cup sugar to replicate the taste.

Looney and Luscious Lemon Squares

This is a great last-minute recipe since most of us have a lemon or two in the house, along with basic baking ingredients.

8 tablespoons Bong Butter (page 14), melted
¼ cup confectioners' sugar
1 cup plus 2 tablespoons all-purpose flour
Pinch of salt
2 large eggs
1 cup granulated sugar
⅓ cup freshly squeezed lemon juice
1 tablespoon grated lemon zest

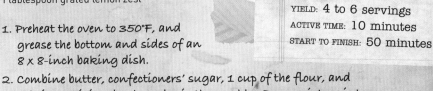

YIELD: 4 to 6 servings
ACTIVE TIME: 10 minutes
START TO FINISH: 50 minutes

1. Preheat the oven to 350°F, and grease the bottom and sides of an 8 x 8-inch baking dish.

2. Combine butter, confectioners' sugar, 1 cup of the flour, and salt in a mixing bowl, and mix thoroughly. Press mixture into the prepared pan. Bake for 20 minutes, or until set and lightly brown. Remove crust from the oven, and set aside.

3. Combine eggs, granulated sugar, remaining 2 tablespoons flour, lemon juice, and lemon zest in a mixing bowl. Beat with an electric mixer on medium speed for 1 minute, or until well blended. Pour topping over crust, and bake for 20 minutes, or until barely brown. The custard should still be soft. Cool the pan on a cooling rack, then cut into 12 pieces.

NOTE: The cookies can be refrigerated for up to 1 week, tightly covered.

VARIATION:
• Substitute lime juice and lime zest for the lemon juice and lemon zest.

Loco Mocha Balls

Whoever decided that chocolate and coffee should have a baby named mocha should get the Nobel Prize in chemistry. These two dark flavors are spectacular together, especially when a goodly amount of Bong Butter is added in.

2 tablespoons instant coffee

2 tablespoons boiling water

8 tablespoons Bong Butter (page 14), softened and cut into small pieces

⅓ cup granulated sugar

1 large egg

½ teaspoon pure vanilla extract

¼ cup unsweetened cocoa powder

1⅓ cups all-purpose flour

Pinch of salt

1 cup confectioners' sugar

YIELD: 4 to 6 servings

ACTIVE TIME: 20 minutes

START TO FINISH: 45 minutes

1. Preheat the oven to 350°F, and grease two baking sheets or cover them with silicon baking mats. Combine coffee powder and water in a small bowl, and stir well to dissolve coffee. Set aside.

Confectioners' sugar contains a small amount of cornstarch, which acts as a binding agent. If you make whipped cream with confectioners' sugar it will not separate as easily as cream beaten with granulated sugar.

2. Combine butter and sugar in a mixing bowl, and beat at medium speed with an electric mixer until light and fluffy. Add egg and vanilla, and beat well. Add cocoa powder and coffee mixture, and beat well, scraping the sides of the bowl as necessary. Reduce the speed to low, and add flour and salt. Beat until just combined.

3. Form dough into 1-inch balls, and place them 1 inch apart on the prepared baking sheets. Bake for 15 to 18 minutes, or until firm. Remove the pans from the oven.

4. Sift confectioners' sugar into a low bowl, and add a few cookies at a time, rolling them around in the sugar to coat them well. Transfer cookies to a rack to cool completely.

NOTE: The cookies can be stored in an airtight container at room temperature up to 3 days, or they can be frozen up to 3 months.

VARIATION:
- For coffee cookies, increase the instant espresso powder to 2 tablespoons and omit the cocoa.

The best way to measure flour is by weighing it; that's the way professional pastry chefs do it. The reason is that how you treat the flour can influence the amount you get. The correct way is to spoon it from the bag into a measuring cup with a spoon, and then level it with a spatula, pushing the extra back into the bag. But what a lot of people do is level it by tapping the measuring cup on the counter. That compresses the flour and you get more than you think.

Boom Bunny Carrot Cookie Sandwiches

These cookies are a hand-holdable version of classic carrot cake, complete with cream cheese frosting holding together the sandwiches. Any bunny would get a good buzz after eating these, and so will you.

1¼ cups all-purpose flour
½ teaspoon ground cinnamon
½ teaspoon ground ginger
½ teaspoon baking soda
¼ teaspoon salt
10 tablespoons Bong Butter (page 14), divided
½ cup firmly packed light brown sugar
½ cup granulated sugar
1 large egg, at room temperature
¾ teaspoon pure vanilla extract, divided
1 cup firmly packed finely grated carrot
¼ cup sweetened coconut
¼ cup finely chopped fresh pineapple
¼ cup raisins
½ cup chopped walnuts, toasted in a 350°F oven for 5 minutes
1 (3-ounce) package cream cheese, softened
1 cup confectioners' sugar

YIELD: 12 cookie sandwiches
ACTIVE TIME: 15 minutes
START TO FINISH: 45 minutes, including 20 minutes for cooling

1. Preheat the oven to 375°F, and grease two baking sheets or line them with silicon baking mats.

2. Sift together flour, cinnamon, ginger, baking soda, and salt. Place 8 tablespoons butter, brown sugar, and granulated sugar in a large mixing bowl. Beat with an electric mixer on low speed to combine, then raise the speed to high and beat for 2 minutes, or until light and fluffy. Add egg and ½ teaspoon vanilla and beat for 2 minutes more. Reduce the speed to low and add

flour mixture until just blended in. Stir in carrot, coconut, pineapple, raisins, and walnuts.

3. Drop batter by rounded tablespoon measures onto the prepared baking sheets, spacing them 2-inches apart; you should have 24 cookies. Bake for 12 to 14 minutes, or until lightly browned. Cool cookies for 1 minute, then transfer cookies with a spatula to a cooling rack and cool completely.

4. While cookies cool, combine cream cheese, confectioners' sugar, remaining 2 tablespoons butter, and remaining ¼ teaspoon vanilla in a food processor fitted with a steel blade or in a mixing bowl. Blend until smooth, and scrape mixture into a mixing bowl.

5. Create cookie sandwiches by spreading frosting on the flat side of 1 cookie and then topping with the flat side of a second cookie. Store at room temperature, tightly covered with plastic wrap.

NOTE: The cookies can be baked up to 2 days in advance and kept at room temperature, tightly covered. They can be filled up to 8 hours in advance.

Flour is always added to a batter last and is only beaten briefly, to keep the cake tender. Flour contains a protein, gluten, that becomes tough if it's overworked. That's why bread dough is kneaded for a long time, so the gluten will allow the yeast to expand, but cakes are mixed for a short period of time.

Gingered Ganja Shortbread Slivers

Shortbread is a classic English cookie that is full of buttery flavor, and in this case the crisp cookies are enlivened with some ganga in the butter as well as crystallized ginger to augment the flavor. These are a perfect cookie to serve with a fruit salad for dessert.

8 tablespoons Bong Butter (page 14), softened
¾ cup granulated sugar
1 teaspoon pure vanilla extract
1 cup all-purpose flour
3 tablespoons cornstarch
¼ cup finely chopped crystallized ginger

Yield: 4 to 6 servings
Active time: 15 minutes
Start to finish: 45 minutes

1. Preheat the oven to 350°F, and grease a 10-inch pie plate.

2. Combine butter, sugar, and vanilla in a mixing bowl, and beat at medium speed with an electric mixer until blended. Increase the speed to high, and beat until light and fluffy. Reduce the speed to low, and add flour, cornstarch, and ginger.

3. Press dough into the prepared pie plate, extending the sides up ½ inch. Cut dough into 12 thin wedges. Prick surface of dough all over with the tines of a fork.

4. Bake for 30 minutes, or until dough is lightly browned at the edges. Remove the pan from the oven, and go over cut lines again. Cool completely on a wire rack, and then remove slivers from the pie plate with a small spatula.

NOTE: The cookies can be made up to 5 days in advance and kept at room temperature in an airtight container.

VARIATIONS:
- Substitute ½ cup miniature chocolate chips for the ginger.
- Substitute ½ cup slivered almonds, toasted in a 350°F oven for 5 to 7 minutes, or until lightly browned, for the ginger, and substitute pure almond extract for the vanilla extract.
- Substitute ½ cup dried cranberries for the ginger, and add 1 tablespoon grated orange zest to the dough.
- Add 1 teaspoon apple pie spice and beat it along with the butter and sugar, and substitute ½ cup raisins for the ginger.

If you're in a hurry to begin a batter, you can grate the butter through the large holes of a box grater. But do not soften butter in a microwave oven. It will become too soft.

Surreal Strawberry Shortcakes

This is an authentic recipe, and the rich and buttery shortcake itself has the texture of a biscuit, in this case a biscuit with a high amount of Bong Butter. You'll never buy those premade sponges in the produce department again!

3 cups all-purpose flour
¾ cup granulated sugar, divided
1 tablespoon cream of tartar
2¼ teaspoons baking soda
¼ teaspoon salt
16 tablespoons Bong Butter (page 14)
2 cups heavy cream, divided
1 quart fresh strawberries
⅓ cup granulated sugar
⅓ cup confectioners' sugar

YIELD: 6 to 8 servings
ACTIVE TIME: 15 minutes
START TO FINISH: 35 minutes

1. Preheat the oven to 375°F, and grease two baking sheets or cover them with silicon baking mats.

2. Combine flour, 1/3 cup sugar, cream of tartar, baking soda, and salt in a medium mixing bowl. Melt 3 tablespoons butter, and set aside. Cut remaining butter into 1/4-inch cubes.

3. Cut butter into flour mixture using a pastry blender, two knives, or your fingertips until mixture resembles coarse meal. Add 1 cup cream, and blend until just blended.

3. Scrape dough onto a floured surface, and knead lightly. Roll dough 3/4-inch thick. Cut out 6 (4-inch) or 8 (3 1/2-inch) rounds, and place them on the baking sheet. Brush rounds with melted butter. Cut out 6 (2 1/2-inch) or 8 (2-inch) rounds and place them on top of larger rounds. Brush tops with butter.

4. Bake for 15 to 17 minutes, or until shortcakes are golden brown. Cool for at least 5 minutes on a wire rack.

5. While shortcakes bake, rinse strawberries, discard green caps, and slice. Toss strawberries with remaining sugar. Set aside. Just prior to serving, whip remaining cream with confectioners' sugar until stiff peaks form.

6. To serve, mound strawberries on larger round, and top with whipped cream and smaller round. Serve immediately.

NOTE: The shortcakes can be prepared up to 2 days in advance and kept at room temperature, tightly covered.

VARIATIONS:
- Substitute blueberries, sliced peaches, or fruit salad for the strawberries.
- Add 2 teaspoons orange zest to the shortcake dough.

We know that strawberries date back to the Roman times, and strawberry shortcakes were already well established when Shakespeare was writing. He mentions them in *The Merry Wives of Windsor*. In the United States, strawberry shortcake parties were popular before the Civil War all over the country because the strawberry was a harbinger of spring.

Crazy Weed Creole Bread Pudding

Pecans and raisins dot this rich, cinnamon-scented warm and wonderful pudding from New Orleans' tradition. It's so homey you want to eat it for breakfast too, and go ahead. A high is a great way to start the day.

½ cup chopped pecans
3 large eggs, lightly beaten and at room temperature
1 cup granulated sugar
1 cup Bhang Booster (page 17)
1 cup half-and-half
8 tablespoons Bong Butter (page 14), melted
1½ teaspoons pure vanilla extract
1 teaspoon ground cinnamon
Pinch of salt
5 cups cubed French bread
½ cup raisins
1 cup Crazy Caramel Sauce (page 84)

YIELD: 6 to 8 servings
ACTIVE TIME: 15 minutes
START TO FINISH: 65 minutes

1. Preheat the oven to 350°F, and grease a 9 x 13-inch baking pan. Place pecans on a baking sheet, and toast in the oven for 5 to 7 minutes, or until browned. Remove the pan from the oven, and set aside.

2. Combine eggs, sugar, Bhang Booster, half-and-half, butter, vanilla, cinnamon, and salt in large mixing bowl, and whisk well. Stir in bread and raisins, and let stand for 10 minutes, or until bread absorbs some of custard, stirring occasionally.

4. Transfer mixture to the prepared pan, and cover with aluminum foil. Bake for 35 minutes, then remove foil, and bake for an additional 10 minutes, or until a knife inserted in the center comes out clean. Cool 5 minutes, then serve, topped with caramel sauce.

Desserts like this one developed as a way to use day-old bread that was a bit stale; in fact, stale bread works better because it absorbs the custard more efficiently. So look for the rack in the supermarket where the bakery breads go when they're a day old. The cost is usually 50 percent less than for fresh bread. And the money you save goes into your stash for stash.

Gooey Pecan Sticky Boom-Boom Buns

Everyone loves a good sticky bun, with lots of buttery caramel and crunchy nuts. But unless you're an insomniac, no one wants to get up at 3 a.m. to get them ready for breakfast. These taste great and you don't have to knead the dough.

Dough

4 large eggs, at room temperature

2 cups lukewarm water

⅓ cup honey

1½ tablespoons instant yeast

2 teaspoons kosher salt

6 tablespoons Bong Butter (page 14), melted and cooled

6½ cups (32 ounces) all-purpose flour, plus additional for dusting

Glaze and Filling

4 cups chopped pecans

12 tablespoons Bong Butter (page 14), melted, divided

YIELD: 8 to 12 servings

ACTIVE TIME: 20 minutes

START TO FINISH: 6 hours, including a total of 5 hours for rising

2½ cups firmly packed light brown sugar, divided

½ cup light corn syrup

3 tablespoons heavy cream

3 teaspoons ground cinnamon

½ teaspoon freshly grated nutmeg

½ teaspoon ground ginger

Vegetable oil spray

1. For dough, place eggs in a large mixing bowl, and beat with a whisk. Add water, honey, yeast, salt, and melted butter, and beat well. Stir in flour with a heavy spoon. Stir for about 1 minute, or until all flour is incorporated. Cover the bowl lightly with a tea towel, and allow it to sit at room temperature for 2 hours, or until doubled in size. Transfer it to the refrigerator for a minimum of 2 hours, and up to 3 days.

2. While dough rises, make the glaze and filling. Preheat the oven to 350ºF. Toast pecans on a baking sheet for 5 to 7 minutes, or until browned.

3. Combine 9 tablespoons of butter, 1½ cups brown sugar, corn syrup, and cream in a small saucepan. Bring to a boil over medium heat, stirring occasionally. Grease 3 (9-inch) round cake pans with vegetable oil spray. Divide glaze into the bottoms of the pans, and tilt the pans to spread the glaze evenly. Sprinkle 1 cup of chopped pecans over the glaze in each pan.

4. For filling, combine remaining pecans, remaining butter, remaining sugar, cinnamon, nutmeg, and ginger in a mixing bowl.

5. Spray your hands with vegetable oil spray. Divide dough into three parts. Sprinkle a counter and rolling pin heavily with flour. Roll dough into a rectangle approximately 10 x 15 inches; this is the size of an average cookie sheet. Sprinkle the rectangle with ⅓ of filling, and roll it beginning with the long side. Cut log into eight pieces, and space them evenly on top of the glaze. Flatten them lightly until they barely touch each other. Repeat with the remaining dough portions and filling.

6. Here are the options at this point:
- Cover the pan lightly with a tea towel, and allow them to rise for 1 hour, or until very puffy. This is if you want to bake them immediately.
- Cover the pans lightly with plastic wrap and refrigerate them. This is if you want to bake them within a day.
- Allow the buns to rise for 1 hour, then cover the pans with foil, and freeze them.

NOTE: The buns can be refrigerated for up to 2 days before baking.

→

7. All options are baked in a preheated 350ºF oven. If buns are sitting at room temperature, bake them for 30 to 35 minutes. If chilled, bake them covered with foil for 10 minutes, then remove the foil and bake them for an additional 25 to 30 minutes. If frozen, bake covered with foil for 20 minutes, and then remove the foil and bake for an additional 20 to 25 minutes. The buns should be brown.

8. Remove the pan or pans from the oven, and invert buns onto a platter. Scrape any glaze remaining in the pan on top of buns, and serve warm.

YIELD: 8 servings
ACTIVE TIME: 20 minutes
START TO FINISH: 2 hours, including time for cooling

Atomic Apple Cake

This moist cake is my answer to taking an apple pie to snack on wherever you go. It has a really moist texture and an intense apple flavor enhanced by aromatic Chinese five-spice powder, which will be even more intense on the second bite once you're high.

Cake

¾ cup raisins

¼ cup rum, treated according to the formulation for Booze with Buzz (page 18)

8 tablespoons Bong Butter (page 14), melted and cooled

2 large eggs, at room temperature

1 cup granulated sugar

2 teaspoons Chinese five-spice powder

1 ½ teaspoons baking powder

½ teaspoon salt

1 ½ cups all-purpose flour

3 Granny Smith apples

Glaze

1 cup confectioners' sugar

3 tablespoons dark rum, treated according to the formulation for Booze with Buzz (page 18)

NOTE: The cake can be prepared up to 1 day in advance and kept at room temperature, loosely covered with plastic wrap.

VARIATIONS:
- Substitute ground cinnamon for the Chinese five-spice powder.
- Substitute dried cranberries or chopped dried apricots for the raisins.

1. Preheat the oven to 350°F. Grease and flour a 10-inch ring pan. Combine raisins and rum in a small microwave-safe bowl, and heat on High (100 percent power) power for 45 seconds. Stir, and allow raisins to plump.

2. Combine butter, eggs, sugar, five-spice powder, baking powder, and salt in a mixing bowl. Whisk by hand until smooth. Add flour, and stir well; the batter will be very thick.

3. Peel, quarter, and core apples. Cut each apple quarter in half lengthwise, and then thinly slice apples. Add apples to batter, and stir to coat apples evenly. Pack batter into the prepared pan.

4. Bake cake in the center of the oven for 1 hour, or until a toothpick inserted in the center comes out clean. Cool cake in the pan set on a cooling rack for 20 minutes, or until cool. Invert cake onto a serving platter.

5. Combine confectioners' sugar and rum in a small bowl. Drizzle glaze over top of cake, allowing it to run down the sides. Serve immediately.

Going Ape Banana Cake

This cake really delivers a banana flavor, and it's also very moist, so no frosting is needed.

1¼ cups mashed very ripe bananas (about 3 bananas)
¾ cup firmly packed light brown sugar
10 tablespoons Bong Butter (page 14), melted
1 large egg, at room temperature
1½ teaspoons baking powder
½ teaspoon ground cinnamon
½ teaspoon salt
1½ cups all-purpose flour

Yield: 6 to 8 servings
Active time: 10 minutes
Start to finish: 45 minutes

1. Preheat the oven to 350°F. Grease and flour an 8 x 8-inch square cake pan.
2. Combine bananas, brown sugar, butter, and egg in a mixing bowl, and whisk vigorously until smooth. Whisk in baking powder, cinnamon, and salt, and then briefly whisk in flour. Scrape batter into the prepared pan, and smooth top with a rubber spatula.
3. Bake cake in the center of the oven for 25 to 30 minutes, or until a toothpick inserted into the center comes out clean. Cool cake in the pan on a cooling rack for 15 minutes. Cut into 6 to 8 portions, and serve warm or at room temperature.

NOTE: The cake can be made up to 2 days in advance and kept at room temperature, lightly covered with plastic wrap.

VARIATION:
- Substitute chopped walnuts or pecans, toasted in a 350°F oven for 5 to 7 minutes or until brown, for the dried apricots.

Baking with bananas might date back to the ancient Greeks. In the fourth century BCE Theophrastus wrote the first book on botany, and it included banana plants. We know that Greeks baked cakes and breads with honey and fruit by the first century CE, so maybe a banana cake was one of them.

YIELD: 6 to 8 servings
ACTIVE TIME: 20 minutes
START TO FINISH: 1¼ hours

Christmas Bud Pear and Gingerbread Upside-Down Cake

This variation on the theme of a cake with fruit on the bottom baked in a skillet is wonderful for fall and winter when pears are in season. The pears really absorb all the caramel richness of the cannabis butter, too.

3 ripe pears

12 tablespoons Bong Butter (page 14), softened, divided

1¼ cups firmly packed light brown sugar, divided

2½ cups all-purpose flour

1½ teaspoons baking soda

1 teaspoon ground cinnamon

1 teaspoon ground ginger

¼ teaspoon ground cloves

¼ teaspoon salt

1 cup molasses

1 cup boiling water

1 large egg, lightly beaten

Vanilla ice cream (optional)

1. Preheat the oven to 350ºF. Peel and core pears, and cut each into 8 wedges. Melt 4 tablespoons butter in a 10-inch cast iron or other ovenproof skillet over medium heat. Reduce heat to low, and sprinkle ¾ cup brown sugar evenly over butter; then cook,

without stirring, for 3 minutes. Not all of sugar will dissolve. Remove the skillet from the heat and arrange pear slices close together on top of brown sugar.

2. Whisk together flour, baking soda, cinnamon, ginger, cloves, and salt in a mixing bowl. Whisk together molasses and boiling water in a small bowl. Combine remaining 8 tablespoons butter, remaining 1/2 cup brown sugar, and egg in a large bowl. Beat with an electric mixer on medium speed for 2 minutes, or until light and fluffy.

3. Reduce mixer speed to low, and add flour mixture in three batches, alternating with molasses mixture, beginning and ending with flour mixture. Beat until just combined. Gently spoon batter over pears, and spread evenly.

4. Bake cake for 40 to 45 minutes, or until golden brown and a cake tester inserted in the center comes out clean. Run a thin knife around the edge of the skillet. Wearing oven mitts, immediately invert a serving plate over the skillet and, holding the skillet and plate together firmly, invert them. Carefully lift off the skillet. If necessary, replace any fruit that might have stuck to the bottom of the skillet on top of the cake. Cool at least 15 minutes or to room temperature before serving, and serve with vanilla ice cream (if using).

NOTE: The cake can be baked up to 8 hours in advance and kept at room temperature.

VARIATION:
- Substitute apples for the pears.

Like bananas, pears ripen better off the tree than they do on it. If you're in a hurry to ripen pears, place them in a plastic bag with a few apples. The apples let off a natural gas that hastens ripening.

YIELD: 8 to 10 servings
ACTIVE TIME: 20 minutes
START TO FINISH: 4 hours, including 2 hours for cake to cool

Maui Wowie Coconut Rum Cake

This cake is like a trip to the tropics while tripping. I'm always in favor of a one-bowl recipe, and this fits the definition. Then the weed-laced cake is soaked in a rum mixture to add additional buzz.

1½ cups sweetened coconut flakes

1¼ cups all-purpose flour

1½ teaspoons baking powder

¼ teaspoon salt

4 large eggs plus 3 large egg yolks

1½ cups granulated sugar

1½ teaspoons pure vanilla extract, divided

12 tablespoons Bong Butter (page 14), melted and cooled

½ cup well-stirred sweetened cream of coconut such as Coco López

½ cup dark rum, treated according to the formulation for Booze with Buzz (page 18)

1 (8-ounce) package cream cheese, softened

3 cups confectioners' sugar

1 teaspoon grated lemon zest

1. Preheat the oven to 375°F. Lightly grease a 9-inch round layer pan, and line the bottom with a round of parchment paper. Lightly grease the parchment paper, and then flour the inside of the pan, tapping out excess flour over the sink.

2. Bake coconut flakes on a baking sheet for 5 to 7 minutes,

114

or until browned. Remove coconut from the oven, and set aside. Reduce the oven temperature to 350°F.

3. Whisk together flour, baking powder, and salt in a small bowl. Whisk together eggs, egg yolks, sugar, and 1 teaspoon vanilla in a large bowl, beating until mixture is thick and lemon-colored. Add 1/2 cup toasted coconut, flour mixture, and butter, and whisk until just combined. Pour batter into the prepared pan, and rap the pan on the counter to expel air bubbles.

4. Bake cake for 45 minutes, or until golden brown and cake starts to pull away from the side of the pan. Cool cake in the pan on a cooling rack for 10 minutes. Invert cake onto the rack and discard parchment. Cool 10 minutes more.

5. Combine cream of coconut and rum in a small bowl, and stir well. Remove 3 tablespoons of mixture, and set aside. Using a meat fork, poke holes in the bottom of cake, and brush coconut rum mixture on the bottom. Allow it to soak in, and repeat. Turn cake over on the rack, and slice off the top so it is level. Spread remaining coconut rum mixture on top, and allow it to soak in. Allow cake to cool completely.

6. For icing, combine cream cheese, confectioners' sugar, remaining 1/2 teaspoon vanilla, lemon zest, and reserved coconut rum mixture in a food processor fitted with the steel blade. Process until smooth, and scrape into a bowl. Apply frosting to cake, and pat remaining 1 cup toasted coconut on the top.

NOTE: The cake can be baked and soaked with the coconut rum mixture up to 2 days in advance and kept at room temperature, tightly covered with plastic wrap. The cake can be frosted up to 1 day in advance and kept at room temperature, lightly covered.

Baking powder does not live forever, and if you haven't used it in a while try this test: Mix 2 teaspoons of baking powder with 1 cup of hot tap water. If there's an immediate reaction of fizzing and foaming, the baking powder can be used. If the reaction is at all delayed or weak, throw the baking powder away and buy a fresh can.

Ganga Ganache Chocolate Nut Torte

The batter for this luscious chocolate cake is created in a matter of minutes in a food processor. It's a dense and rich cake that is crunchy with nuts and topped with a candy-like ganache.

10 ounces bittersweet chocolate, chopped, divided

2 cups pecan or walnut halves, toasted in a 350°F oven for 5 minutes

2 tablespoons plus ½ cup granulated sugar

16 tablespoons Bong Butter (page 14), softened, divided

3 large eggs, at room temperature

1 tablespoon rum, treated according to the formulation for Booze with Buzz (page 18)

YIELD: 8 to 10 servings
ACTIVE TIME: 15 minutes
START TO FINISH: 1½ hours, including 1 hour for chilling

1. Preheat the oven to 375°F. Grease a 9-inch round cake pan, cut out a circle of waxed paper or parchment to fit the bottom, and grease the paper.

2. Melt 4 ounces chocolate in a microwave oven or over simmering water in a double boiler. Cool slightly. Reserve 12 nut halves and chop the remaining nuts with 2 tablespoons sugar in a food processor fitted with a steel blade, using on-and-off pulsing. Scrape nuts into a bowl. Beat 8 tablespoons butter and remaining ½ cup sugar in the food processor until light and fluffy. Add melted chocolate, then add eggs, 1 at a time. Beat well between each addition, and scrape the sides of the work bowl with a rubber spatula. Add rum, then fold chocolate mixture into ground nuts.

3. Scrape batter into the prepared pan and bake for 25 minutes. The cake will be soft but will firm up as it cools. Remove cake from the oven and cool 20 minutes on a cooling rack. Invert cake onto a plate, remove the paper, and cool completely.

4. To make glaze, combine remaining 6 ounces chocolate and remaining 8 tablespoons butter in a small saucepan. Melt over low heat and beat until shiny and smooth. Place cake on a rack over a sheet of wax paper. Pour the glaze onto the center of the cake, and rotate the rack at an angle so glaze runs down sides of the cake. Top with the nut halves, and allow to sit in a cool place until chocolate hardens.

NOTE: The cake can be prepared 1 day in advance and refrigerated. Allow it to reach room temperature before serving.

VARIATIONS:
- Add 1 tablespoon instant espresso powder to the batter.
- Substitute Triple Sec or Grand Marnier for the rum, and add 2 teaspoons grated orange zest to the batter.
- Substitute blanched almonds for the pecans or walnuts, substitute amaretto for the rum, and add ½ teaspoon pure almond extract to the batter.

Because chocolate can absorb aromas and flavors from other foods, it should always be wrapped tightly after being opened. Store chocolate in a cool, dry place, but not in the refrigerator or freezer. If stored at a warm temperature, the fat will rise to the surface and become a whitish powder called a bloom. It will disappear, however, as soon as the chocolate is melted. Chocolate, like red wines, ages and becomes more deeply flavored after six months.

INDEX

Hooched Up Hot Banana Splits
with Chocolate Sauce, 88

Kona Gold Coconut Chocolate Fudge, 71

Linguine in Creamy Cannibis
Tomato Sauce, 48

Lobo Lemon Chicken, 60

Loco Mocha Balls, 96

Looney and Luscious Lemon Squares, 95

Magic Mushroom Quesadillas, 52

Maple Raisin Reefer Rice Pudding, 80

Maui Wowie Coconut Rum Cake, 114

Ode to Alice B. Toklas
Marble Fudge Brownies, 90

Outrageous Onion Pizza Niçoise
(Pissaladière), 38

Panzanella with Punch, 45

Pasta with Jolly Green Garlic and Oil
(Pasta Aglio e Olio), 50

Penuche, 70

Pot-Filled Potato Puffs, 33

Power of Pepper Pasta Carbonara, 64

Rasta Weed Chicken Wraps, 62

Shrimp Scampi with Swag, 51

So Sweet and So Salty Tapenade, 23

Souped-Up Cereal Mix, 30

Spicy Spiked Cornmeal Muffins, 40

DINNER GUEST LIST

MENU NOTES...

FAVORITES

Also by DR. SEYMOUR KINDBUD
and Cider Mill Press

Green Weed:
The Organic Guide
to Growing
High-Quality Cannibus
$19.95
978-1604331578

The Little Green
Book of Weed
$9.95
978-1604331769

Happy (Happy!!!) Holiday Pot Cookie-Swap Cookbook

$12.95

978-1604332384

Grow Your Own Organic Weed: Everything You Need... Except the Seeds

$9.95

978-1604332322

Pot Stickers

$12.95

978-1604332001

About Cider Mill Press
Book Publishers

Good ideas ripen with time. From seed
to harvest, Cider Mill Press brings fine
reading, information, and entertainment
together between the covers of its
creatively crafted books. Our Cider Mill
bears fruit twice a year, publishing a new
crop of titles each spring and fall.

**Visit us on the Web at
www.cidermillpress.com**
or write to us at
12 Port Farm Road
Kennebunkport, Maine 04046